STARTING A
HOUSE
CHURCH

Larry Kreider
& Floyd McClung

Regal

From Gospel Light
Ventura, California, U.S.A.

Published by Regal Books
From Gospel Light
Ventura, California, U.S.A.
Printed in the U.S.A.

Regal Books is a ministry of Gospel Light, a Christian publisher dedicated to serving the local church. We believe God's vision for Gospel Light is to provide church leaders with biblical, user-friendly materials that will help them evangelize, disciple and minister to children, youth and families.

It is our prayer that this Regal book will help you discover biblical truth for your own life and help you meet the needs of others. May God richly bless you.

For a free catalog of resources from Regal Books/Gospel Light, please call your Christian supplier or contact us at 1-800-4-GOSPEL *or* www.regalbooks.com.

Library of Congress Cataloging-in-Publication Data
Kreider, Larry.
Starting a house church / Larry Kreider & Floyd McClung.
    p. cm.
ISBN 0-8307-4365-0 (trade paper)
1. House churches. I. McClung, Floyd. II. Title.
BV601.85.K74 2007
254'.1—dc22   2006034897

1 2 3 4 5 6 7 8 9 10 / 10 09 08 07

Rights for publishing this book in other languages are contracted by Gospel Light Worldwide, the international nonprofit ministry of Gospel Light. Gospel Light Worldwide also provides publishing and technical assistance to international publishers dedicated to producing Sunday School and Vacation Bible School curricula and books in the languages of the world. For additional information, visit www.gospellightworldwide.org; write to Gospel Light Worldwide, P.O. Box 3875, Ventura, CA 93006; or send an e-mail to info@gospellightworldwide.org.

CONTENTS

SPECIAL THANKS

We really enjoyed writing this book together. We could not have done it without Karen Ruiz, our editor and writing assistant from Partnership Publications. Thank you, Karen, for sharing your expertise with us. Great job! Thanks also to Peter Bunton for all of his valuable input. And a special thanks to Bill Greig III, Gary Greig, Kim Bangs and the entire Regal team. You have been wonderful to work with. And finally, we are so grateful to the Lord for our amazing wives, LaVerne Kreider and Sally McClung, our partners in life and ministry.

Larry Kreider
Floyd McClung

WHY HOUSE CHURCHES?

There are over three billion people on our planet who have never heard the name of Jesus one time, and there are thousands of people groups that have not been reached with the good news of God's love. Poverty, corruption, preventable diseases and famine have turned entire countries and continents to ruin. As followers of Christ, we are stirred to face these challenges with both faith in God's goodness and obedience to His commands.

We believe the Church is the hope of the world. Some would say this statement leaves out Jesus, that He alone is the hope of the world. Not at all! Jesus Himself chose the Church to be His answer to the world's needs.

We also believe that the Church has been commissioned to respond with Jesus' compassion and the good news of the Cross to both the physical and spiritual challenges the world faces. We believe in sharing God's love with two hands—one hand with food, medicine and clean water, and the other hand with the message of God's love.

Because we love the Church and have served her for a total of 70 years, we are in no way prepared to give up on her. She has needs. She has weaknesses. And yes, she is hopeless without Jesus. But she is His bride—His family—and we love her because of that. We love the whole Church, big and small, black and white, rich and poor, young and old. So neither one of us is writing this book to present the one answer to the Church's problems.

We are excited about house churches, but not to the exclusion of the rest of the Body of Christ. If you are looking for a book that hammers and criticizes the institutional Church or denominations or mega-churches, this is the wrong book for you. Rather, we are excited about how God's Spirit is moving through house churches to touch our planet. Most of the people who have never heard the good news about Jesus live in countries that are closed to traditional expressions of Sunday-oriented, building-driven churches. What is happening around the world right now through house-church movements is spectacular. Already, tens of millions of people are coming to Christ through hundreds of thousands of small, simple churches in Africa, Asia and Latin America. We pray that our own nation and the nations of the developing world begin to experience the same blessing.

If we are going to reach the three billion unreached people of our planet who live in small villages and crowded cities, it will not be through program-driven, professional-clergy models of Western church. There is probably no more significant factor in the growth of the Church worldwide than the recently rediscovered power of small, simple, easily reproducible churches.

The principles that make small, simple churches work well are not only fueling worldwide church growth but are also helping people grow spiritually. Home churches produce ownership, accountability, spontaneity, involvement, responsibility and growth among attendees. We will explain more about these principles later on in the book.

We believe that God has a big dream for the Church—but He builds His Church one life, one family and one small church community at a time. We, too, should dream big dreams while we build small. The maturity and effectiveness of *any* movement of lasting impact can be measured by how effective it is in fostering a culture of small groups that can function as a church for the people.

To clarify, it is not a particular model of church that motivates us, but what the Spirit of God does in people's lives when they discover the New Testament principles of doing Church in small communities. It is those principles that form the engine that powers the house-church model, not the model itself. These principles are not complicated, and figuring them out doesn't require a seminary education. The New Testament principles are woven throughout the story of the Church in the book of Acts, and they continue today to permeate the house-church movement worldwide.

With this in mind, we offer you our stories, our experiences and the lessons we have learned, with the hope that they will guide and inspire you to see what God does when you open your home, your office or your classroom to a few other people.

Larry Kreider
www.dcfi.org; www.startingahousechurch.com

Floyd McClung
www.floydandsally.com

CHAPTER 1

THERE'S A NEW KIND OF CHURCH EMERGING!

It's happening again. A new species of church is emerging throughout North America. In major cities and in rural areas, unique expressions of church are breaking through the soil like new plants in the spring. These churches are diverse in theology and method. They have different names and involve different generations. They are different sizes and meet in a variety of places. Yet each one is an expression of the Church—the Body of Christ.

Some meet in homes, others meet in art galleries, coffee shops, warehouses, fast-food restaurants, industrial complexes, parks, and other unconventional places. Some are called "house churches," others are dubbed "micro-churches," "simple churches" or "organic churches," and still others prefer not to be branded at all. Some have structure; others avoid structure as if it were a disease.

Although these new expressions of church are just beginning to dot the landscape of North America, they already cover the landscapes of other nations around the world. Places like China, Central Asia, Latin America, India and Cambodia have experienced tremendous growth through small, simple churches that disciple and empower participants to be "the Church."

Hungry for community and relationship, people involved in this spontaneous movement around the world are learning the values of the Kingdom by firsthand participation. Church becomes a way of life: Discipleship and growth occur naturally, as everyone develops his or her gifts and learns by doing under the mentoring of spiritual fathers and mothers.

Some religious historians believe that house churches represent the next wave of evangelical worship, after the boom in megachurches that occurred during the 1980s and 1990s. The trend was recently captured in an article in *Time* magazine, which describes how "evangelicals are abandoning mega churches for mini churches, based in their own living rooms."[1] Pollster George Barna has found that 5 percent of all believers in America are currently involved in house churches—and the trend is growing rapidly.[2]

House churches work so that each small church functions as a little church. Often they network with other micro-churches for accountability and encouragement from others with the same passions. Although these small churches seem to be a rapidly growing contemporary trend, house churches are not really new; in fact, they are as old as the book of Acts.

The New Testament church, the church encountered in the book of Acts, was defined as *people*. Believers did not *go* to church or *join* the church—they *were* the Church. Unlike the Old Testament system that consisted of a few priests, all the members in the New Testament church functioned as priests, because everyone served with the abilities and gifts God gave them. These followers of Christ practiced their faith in spiritual families, met in homes and radically changed their world. In this context, each person learned how to mentor others. The believers grew in number as they obeyed God's Word and shared resources and spiritual blessings. Thus, the New Testament church formed the original movement of house churches.

The Constant Need for New Expressions

Although there are already thousands upon thousands of healthy, vibrant churches throughout North America and the world, new expressions of church are continually needed to accommodate believers who do not fit into the current church structures. Just as wine can be contained in both bottles and glasses, so God's Church necessitates many different sizes and shapes of containers. Jesus referred to this problem of "wineskins" in His day. He taught that new wine needs new wineskins, because old, brittle wineskins will burst with the fermentation of new wine (see Luke 5:37).

Just like the generations before them, many of today's young people look at the existing wineskins and have no enthusiasm for them. During the past five years, in our discussions with young men and women throughout North America and in various nations, we hear repeatedly, "I love Jesus. I respect sincere followers of Jesus. I am not rebellious, but I just feel like I want a new, non-churchy way of doing things, something I can give myself to." Young people are looking for a church experience in which they can enthusiastically participate.

It is not just the younger generation that backs away from full participation in church life. Older people, too, are looking for a new model of church in which they can be fully involved. For example, one man in his 50s once confided with tears running down his cheeks, "I know the Lord called me years ago to be a pastor, but I just do not know how it can ever happen here in my church." This man, a loving pastoral person who put relationships first, was longing to fulfill God's call on his life. Think what could happen if he had a micro-church venue. As a spiritual father in a house church, he could fulfill his heart's cry. In a house church, he could look after his spiritual extended family and find his niche.

Even though simple community appeals to people across the generations, we believe that overall, the younger generation will take the lead in starting new house churches and house-church networks in our communities. Why? Because this generation, with little or no formal attachment to church, is in need of a new wineskin that fits its need for authentic relationships. Since the next generation is looking for dependable, meaningful relationships, young adults are very open to small groups that are based on friendships and socializing. They love to spend time hanging out. Young people in the next generation especially crave real-life connections because they were raised in the non-physically oriented communication structures of cyberspace:

> Our culture once based exclusively on physical contact is being transformed to one where goods and services are accessible without face-to-face contact with other people. Technology enables this transformation.[3]

Although the Internet creates an online "community," with e-mail, instant messaging, blogs, news groups and the ability to run a home business on the Web, it is missing the vital element of physical human contact. Technology, however helpful (PCs, PDAs, cell phones and a multitude of other gadgets at our fingertips), does not inspire the deep relational connections that the next generation is seeking.

Impacting the Culture

God wants to change how we view church. He loves the old but injects new life into His Church through those people who are courageous enough to honor the old while they do the new.

As a young man, I (Floyd) read and dreamt a lot about radical Christian community; but it wasn't until I took courage and lived my dream that I discovered the new things God wanted to teach me. I grew up in a church tradition that, I felt, was out of touch with the world. As a young visionary, I became suspicious of institutional structures and religious leaders who could preach fiery sermons but who were not marching in the streets against the injustices I saw in the world. I wanted to face the future with imagination and courage, but the church traditions I grew up with encouraged believers to react against anyone who challenged the Church status quo.

In reaction to my church's traditionalism, my wife, Sally, and I saw ourselves as part of the same revolution that Jesus and the Early Church started. We were unafraid to critique institutional Church traditions even though we weren't sure where the revolution was leading us. While my friends and I took part in civil rights demonstrations, my church seemed intent on drawing up more rules—so I left.

My journey led me, eventually, to start a street ministry for dropped-out young people. I signed up with a Christian organization that was mobilizing young people to go to the nations. I wanted a challenge and they gave it to me. Sally and I led a street ministry in those days, which meant rousing our converts out of bed on Sunday mornings so that they could "go to church." Unfortunately, the churches didn't know what to do with our long-haired, tattooed and pierced disciples; it was a battle every Sunday morning. I experienced a growing disillusionment with this practice of church-going. Church as Sally and I experienced it, one morning a week, was not relevant to the lives of the young people with whom we were working. I was deeply frustrated.

Then, a Bible teacher came to conduct a seminar for us. After he saw what we were doing, he commended us for the many young people we were leading to Christ, but he asked why we didn't gather them and start an alternative church. He said, "You are blessing many young people, Floyd; but what are you building?" When I asked him what he meant, he talked about the responsibility of being a spiritual father to the young people who were coming to Christ through our ministry. I was barely old enough to vote; how was I was to be their father? He told me that Sally and I should not expect others to take care of those we were leading to Christ; he challenged us to gather them in small groups and also, as we were able, to gather in celebrations. He called this process "building," in contrast to "blessing." He told me that doing ministry without a clear aim—to build a healthy community—was irresponsible. He said that God had something better in mind. He challenged me to build, lead and care for a discipling community that would, in turn, become part of God's worldwide mission.

I wish I could tell you there was a quick and radical breakthrough in my experience. There wasn't. My journey was marked by many stops and starts. I made a lot of mistakes. Fortunately, God helped me to learn from my errors. One of the things I did commit to during that time was to vow to do nothing that did not lead to the start of new church communities. This included short-term outreaches. This produced the most amazing results. Sally and I started churches among the prostitutes and in unreached neighborhoods. We sent teams to other countries, including "closed" countries. We were amazed at how open people were to Jesus-oriented community who were not open to Christianity as a religion. Eventually, a movement called All Nations grew out of our efforts to reach people who had never heard the good news. Scores of new churches sprang up in Central Asia, Russia, India, Mongolia and Greece as a result.

One leader, whom we discipled in a small Bible study, went on to start a movement of churches that has grown to more than 40 congregations in several nations. Another young man we invested in had an impact on the youth of a whole nation through music and arts festivals that are now influencing tens of thousands of unchurched young people.

What Sally and I built was unconventional, not unbiblical. We got in touch with God's desire for His people to impact the culture. Through our efforts, we encountered the reason for our existence. I believe now that we were tapping into the primal

Spirit-led urging for the good news to be given to the world. I believe that God wanted us to reach the outsiders rather than coddle the insiders. In the end, we stumbled on the outward-focused calling of the Church as God's missional people. What beat in our hearts then is the same stirring that is in the hearts of many emerging leaders now. It is a latent desire, stirred by the Holy Spirit, for the *ecclesia* to be unleashed. It is the creative presence of the Holy Spirit yearning for a community of people who will engage our culture. It is the Spirit calling us to live the gospel *within* our culture, rather than perpetuate churchy institutions that exist *apart* from our culture.

Each Generation Must Find Its Fit

Every generation needs the freedom to discover and discern which wineskin is best for it. Here's how Leonard Sweet explains it in his book *Aqua Church*:

> My wife is a tea drinker. Her favorite container is a little cup with a handle so tiny I can't even get my finger through it. My favorite container is a Jadite coffee mug (I started collecting Fire King Jadite long before Martha Stewart inflated the market and made it uncollectible). Our eight-year-old Thane's favorite container is a little glass we put juice in. Our three-year-old Soren's favorite container is a Winnie the Pooh sippy cup. Eighteen-month-old Egil's favorite container is a bottle.
>
> Every generation needs a shape that fits its own hands, its own soul. Each generation, every person, needs a different handle from which to receive the living waters of Jesus. Our task is to pour the living water into anything anyone will pick up. By "anything," I mean that literally: anything. If I want to reach my twenty-second-

century children (they probably will live to see 2100) with the gospel of Jesus, I must be prepared to pour the living water into containers of which I myself would never be caught dead drinking. This is what Paul meant when he talked about our "becoming all things to all men" that we might win some (1 Corinthians 9:22).[4]

Once again, today's generation needs a unique "shape that fits its hands." However, they need to be released to find that shape. After speaking at a leadership conference in a large church in the United States, a woman said to me (Larry):

Every week my home is filled with a twenty-something crowd of young people. They are not the kind of kids that fit in the traditional church. I know they are experiencing Church right in my home, but I do not want to be competitive to my church or be misunderstood. However, I see that we are becoming *the Church* as a body of believers.

Many others face this same dilemma. They are experiencing dynamic church community in a home, but they need to be released to really *be* the Church.

A new wineskin is emerging; let's not resist it. It may change the look of church as we know it, but let's open our hearts so that the new and the old can work together. Let's release the emerging churches and allow them to find their places in the transformation of our families, our cities and our nations!

Notes

1. Rita Healy and David Van Biema, "There's No Pulpit Like Home," *Time* magazine, March 6, 2006.
2. George Barna, *Revolution* (Wheaton, IL: Tyndale House Publishers, 2005), p. 49.
3. Paul Gray and Magid Igbaria, "The Virtual Society," *OR/MS Today*, December 1996, p. 44.
4. Leonard Sweet, *Aqua Church* (Loveland, CO: Group, 1999), pp. 28-29.

CHAPTER 2

DIFFERENT KINDS OF CHURCHES FOR DIFFERENT KINDS OF PEOPLE

My wife, LaVerne, and I (Larry), with a team of young leaders, hauled the young people we were mentoring by the vanload to every church imaginable in our south-central Pennsylvania community in order to find a suitable church where they could fit in. But it was the classic case of a square peg being forced into a round hole: They just didn't fit. The new believers we were trying to integrate into some of the local churches in our communities complained of feeling out of place and disconnected. It was the late 1970s, and many young people felt that the Church in general was out of touch with popular culture.

What were we to do, then, with the dozens of unchurched young people who were coming to faith in Christ? We decided to start a new church—a different kind of church that gave everyone the opportunity to contribute something—where participants could explore issues of faith, the media, culture, relationships, career and social action in a family-type gathering or small-group setting. The new cell-based church that grew out of this need started in the early 1980s and embodied what I thought was a radical outlook on doing church. We met in small cell groups during the week and held a large celebration on Sunday mornings. As we outgrew our building on Sunday mornings, we began to meet each week in multiple sites and to all come together to celebrate the life of Christ at one large gymnasium or park every few months. The church grew during the next 10 years to more than 2,300 people.

As we grew, we realized that if we wanted to build the Church with a cell-group focus in the nations of the world, we would have to give the church away. So we did exactly that. We decentralized our church in south-central Pennsylvania in 1996, and became eight cell-based churches. Out of this change, we birthed a growing church-planting movement called DOVE Christian Fellowship International (DCFI) and soon had churches planted in 15 nations.

However, after several years it became apparent that there was a sense of unrest in our growing church. I especially noticed this with some of the young people. They craved a new type of wineskin that would provide a more contemporary venue in which to get involved. They were saying the same kind of things we had said years earlier: "We're looking for something new. We need something that truly meets our needs." Our wineskin had begun to age—it was past its prime for many of the younger generation.

It didn't take long for us to conclude that we had to find ways to plant new churches (new wineskins) and that we would have to begin the process of handing the reins over to the next generation. If we didn't, we would lose what we already had.

Could it be that God wants to change everything about how we view the Church? He has created the Church to be a dynamic, growing, changing movement, not a static doctrine. The Spirit of God calls each generation to re-imagine church for its own context and culture. The Holy Spirit invites every generation into the struggle to discover answers and approaches for themselves about church—answers that bring them into fresh partnership with God and fresh contact with their culture.

Containers Have Their Limitations

What would you say is the best container to hold water—a glass or a bottle? The truth is that each container is unique, and each has its limitations, depending on the situation. Bottled water makes sense if you are on the move, taking a long walk and needing sips at regular intervals. A glass is more practical if you are sitting at the dinner table. If we insisted that bottles are the only containers worthy to hold water, you might think us a bit deranged—and rightly so! Different containers serve different purposes, just as different kinds of churches serve different kinds of people.

It is not wise to become too dogmatic about a particular model of church—the *container*. Often, in our zeal, when we believe that God has shown us something new, we have a tendency to go overboard. We tout *our* container as the one and only way to do church. We start the Container denomination and write books about Containers. Then we start a Container school. And of course we eventually franchise the product, because we are Americans! Actually, it's not the kind of container, its size or its label that counts—it's what is on the inside. And by the time we brand and sell our container, God uses a different container to accomplish His purposes!

Rest assured—we are not writing this book because we have found the right formula or correct model of doing church. One model does not fit all—the model that works for us is not the answer for everyone. Neither are we trying to fix the Church—God is not calling us to focus on changing people in existing churches nor those churches they are a part of. Rather, we believe that the Lord is using diversified structures to build His Church today. From the traditional church to the emerging house-church networks, God's Spirit is being poured out on *all* His people.

That being said, we believe that the micro-church is just one among the best containers to accomplish God's purpose.

It is a container that is simple, easily multiplied, involves everyone, releases leadership and produces accountability. We are impressed with that which will accomplish the greatest glory to God and the greatest growth in people's lives, and micro-churches fall into that category.

Likewise, God is still using today's conventional church structures—what we call the community churches and mega-churches—to play their part in His future plan. We sincerely believe that the new house churches are tailor-made for today's generation, but we also know that God will build His kingdom regardless of our models, structures or plans.

Both those churches that operate within a more traditional setting and those that operate outside of traditional structures are needed. It is a big job to equip the saints for ministry and bring the good news to the world. We need everyone to work together, allowing the new and the old to coexist and even complement each other. Their combined strengths will contribute to advancing God's kingdom here on Earth.

The Community Church

Community Churches Like a community store
Mega-churches
House-Church Networks

In nearly every city around the world, you can find what we call "community churches." Most of these churches meet in a church facility each Sunday morning, in addition to holding various meetings at the church building throughout the week. There are many styles and flavors of community churches. There is the Methodist flavor, the Baptist flavor, the Congregational flavor, the Episcopal flavor, the Presbyterian flavor, the Vineyard flavor, the Assembly of God flavor, the nondenominational flavor, the independent flavor—the list goes on and on. Some are Calvinist. Some are Arminian. Some are Charismatic in their worship expression, while some are traditional. Some churches are theologically dispensational, while others focus on the here and now. Some churches are cell-based. Some are "seeker-sensitive," geared toward those new to following Christ, while others appeal to the mature Christian with extended times of worship and the exercising of spiritual gifts. We love the many unique expressions of the Body of Christ. It would be boring if each expression looked exactly the same!

My family and I (Larry) live in rural Lancaster County, Pennsylvania. In this county alone, there are more than 600 community churches—of every kind imaginable. The great majority of the churches in our county have between 50 and 200 members. Some have 400 to 500 or even 800 to 900 regular attendees. Although community churches range in size, they all have a clear target area: the local populace. In many cases, those who attend and those whom the community churches reach live in the general geographical area.

Community Churches Are Like Community Stores

The community church reminds us of the local community store. Where do you buy your groceries? You probably shop at a local grocery store in your community. It might be an independent store or it could be part of a large chain. You may personally know the clerks and where specific items are shelved. Some neighborhood stores are larger than others—you may even walk to a corner grocery store.

You go to the community store because it's a short distance from where you live. Likewise, community churches are places that serve your local area, offering that small-town feel. In the same way that very few people in your neighborhood would drive a long distance to get their groceries, very few people are willing to drive long distances to worship with other believers who gather each week at churches that aren't local. Proximity and ease of access are as big a part of the nature of the community church as they are of community grocery stores.

Thirty years ago, nearly every church in America was a community church (generally, a church of 50 to 1,000 in attendance). Then something happened. American Christians and American pastors started to hear reports about churches in places like Seoul, Korea, that were massive. We heard that there were more than 100,000 people in Yoido Full Gospel Church in Seoul. (Since then, this church has grown much larger: 2003 statistics revealed that there were 780,000 members.) [1]

Dr. Yonggi Cho, pastor of the world's largest church in Seoul, came to America to explain how pastors could also have large churches by "praying and obeying." He taught church leaders to obey the voice of the Holy Spirit and to train small-group (cell) leaders and release the ministry of the Church into their hands. With the help of small groups, rapid multiplication and growth occurred.

The Mega-church

Community Churches Like a community store
Mega-churches Like a Wal-Mart Superstore
House-Church Networks

The new mentality that emerged during the late twentieth century led to a tidal wave of mega-churches across urban and rural
America. Many of these churches implemented cell groups to
help them grow. For example, Victory Christian Center, founded in Tulsa, Oklahoma, by pastor Billy Joe Daugherty, grew into
a mega-church due, in part, to the cell groups they fostered for
more than 25 years.

Today, at least in the United States, it is not unusual for people to drive for an hour or more to attend worship services at a
mega-church. Mega-churches have much to offer. There are
ministries for every member of the family, 12-step programs for
those with addictions, Bible schools, concerts, youth ministries,
singles' ministries—you name it, almost anything is available.
This kind of large church with its expansive programs appeals
to "baby boomers and others who enjoy the polished nature of
the worship services, and who find the size and the upbeat style
of these churches appealing."[2]

The mega-church phenomenon has changed the face of
the Church in America. Popular Bible teacher and bishop T. D.
Jakes started his mega-church when he relocated his and 50
other families from West Virginia to Dallas, Texas. The new
church was called The Potter's House. Within 18 months, it
grew to more than 14,000 worshipers! It is one of the nation's
fastest-growing mega-churches. *Christianity Today* magazine
noted that "other mega-churches such as Saddleback Valley
Community Church in Mission Viejo, California, and Willow
Creek in South Barrington, Illinois, took several years to become so large."[3]

It is a fact that mega-churches are growing rapidly. According
to a 2005 survey conducted by Hartford Seminary's Hartford
Institute for Religion Research, "at latest count, there are 1,210
Protestant churches in the United States with weekly attendance
over 2,000, nearly double the number that existed 5 years ago."[4]

Mega-churches Are Like Wal-Mart Superstores

For just a moment, let's call the mega-church the "Wal-Mart superstore church." Wal-Mart has taken the U.S. by storm. Twenty-five years ago, Wal-Mart was a department store chain located primarily in the southern part of our nation. Now Wal-Mart is everywhere! People will drive for hours to shop at a Wal-Mart, because they love the low prices, the huge inventory of consumer products and the fact that they can get all they need in one place at one time.

Mega-churches, like the Wal-Mart superstores, are large and offer an abundance of services to the churchgoer. Like Wal-Mart superstores, everything is easily accessible in one location. However, unlike the community church where a member may know nearly everyone, a mega-churchgoer is likely to know only a few people. Everyone has varying needs, so it's not unusual that some people love Wal-Mart while others seldom—if ever—shop there. The same is true when people decide which church to attend. Some love the mega-church, while others feel lost in the crowd and prefer the smaller community church.

In 1980, I (Larry) started pastoring a church that focused on meeting in home-based cell groups during the week and also in Sunday morning services. Using the cell-group structure, we continued to multiply our numbers until we were in the mega-church category. Many of us drove an hour or more to attend weekly services on Sunday. There was a Bible school, a dynamic youth ministry, a singles' ministry and a ministry for those who had gone through a divorce; dozens of short-term mission teams were sent out, and many other specialized ministries were taking place. Dr. Cho, the pastor of the world's largest church, even came to speak at our church for a leadership conference. Our mega-church had the feel of a spiritual Wal-Mart, and I loved my time there. But I also understand that different forms of church appeal to different people. While the mega-church lifestyle appealed to me in my previous pastoral days, and though I am able to appreciate certain aspects of community churches, there is much to say about house-church networks, as well.

House-Church Networks

Community Churches Like a community store
Mega-churches Like a Wal-Mart Superstore
House-Church Networks Like a Shopping Mall with Many Stores

A few years ago, I (Larry) agreed to home-school my then 16-year-old son, Josh. Had I told you 35 years ago that I was going to home-school my son, you'd probably think I was involved in some type of new cult. If you recall, home-schooling was almost unheard of in America at that time. Nevertheless, early home-schooling advocates made their mark on education in America, and today the practice is commonplace and well accepted as an alternative to traditional classroom training. Parents today have the choice of home-schooling their children or sending them to public or private schools. All three types of educational training coexist in nearly every community in America.

We believe that within the next several years, house-church networks will—as the home-schooling phenomenon did in the 1980s and '90s—mushroom all across America. Like our educational choices, they will coexist and network with community churches and mega-churches that meet in traditional church buildings in our communities every Sunday. Our belief is that God will use and bless all three—the community churches, the mega-churches and the house-church networks. While the community church may be compared to a community store and the mega-church to a Wal-Mart superstore, a house-church network is analogous to stores in a shopping mall. If the average store found in a shopping mall was taken out of the mall to stand on its own, it would die within a year— each specialized store flourishes only within the cluster of the others. The normal store in a shopping mall needs the other stores to survive, yet each store remains a "store" in its own right, despite its larger context within a mall.

House churches function like these shopping mall stores— they are individual and specialized, yet they can only thrive when they network together with other house churches. We will explain later how they network, but for now let's look at how each one functions as a real church.

House Churches Have a Unique Mentality

The entire concept of house churches requires a different way of thinking than we have been used to. Believers in these micro-churches do not focus on growing larger like the community church or the mega-church. They focus on growth by multiplication into new house churches.

House churches are small and therefore can meet anywhere— in a house, a college dorm room, a coffee shop or a corporate boardroom. They meet in these locations and do not think of growing larger, which would require the construction of a building to accommodate the larger group. Instead, they say, "How can we multiply leaders and start more house churches?" and "How can we walk together as house-church leaders?"

DAWN, a "saturation" church-planting ministry (a ministry that aims at mobilizing the whole Body of Christ within an area, city, province or country to plant a church within easy access of every person in order to disciple the whole nation), further clarifies this very point:

> The house church is a structure that reflects the core nature of the church . . . It is a spiritual, enlarged, organic family . . . It is inherently participatory and not consumer-provider driven. Its responsibility structure is also very simple and effective: individual house churches are fathered by elders, who in turn are equipped by itinerant servants like those in the fivefold ministry (see Eph. 4:11-13). They often relate to a regional spiritual father-figure, who, through his humble apostolic passion and vision, often becomes some thing like a "pillar of the church," an anchor-place for a regional movement that fills its cities and villages with the presence of Christ . . . The church is the people of God. The church, therefore, was and is at home where people are at home: in ordinary houses.[5]

It's Time to "Pray and Obey" Again

Time marches on. What was new and unique several years ago becomes an old wineskin in today's world. We believe it is time again to pray and obey. Today's generation is dreaming of another type of church in America—the house church.

In today's church world, you can find the community store churches and the Wal-Mart superstore churches everywhere. The Lord has and will continue to use them. However, He will also use the new house churches, with their different approaches and structures, to build His kingdom. Let's open our hearts to this revolutionary force that is growing quietly in humble house churches across the nation. These miniature expressions of the Body of Christ have the potential to revitalize and rapidly expand the Church of Jesus Christ in America.

Notes
  1. Wikipedia, "Megachurch," July 2006. http://en.wikipedia.org/wiki/Megachurch (accessed December 2006).
  2. Ibid.
  3. Jim Jones, "Swift Growth Shapes Potter's House," *Christianity Today*, January 12, 1998, vol. 42, No. 1, p. 56.
  4. Scott Thumma, Dave Travis and Warren Bird, "Megachurches Today 2005: Summary of Research Findings," February 2006, Hartford Institute for Religious Research, Hartford Seminary, Hartford Connecticut. http://hirr.hartsem.edu/org/faith_megachurches_research.html (accessed December 2006).
  5. "The Church Comes Home," *DAWN Report*, August 1999, pp. 1-2.

CHAPTER 3

THE MOST EFFECTIVE WAY TO EVANGELIZE: START NEW CHURCHES

The two *primary* focuses of healthy house churches are outreach and discipleship, rather than fellowship alone. This is because the biblical focus of the Church is outreach and discipleship. Great fellowship *is* a healthy by-product of the house church that consistently reaches out to others—but it cannot be the goal if you want your house church to fully please God.

Prayer and interaction are encouraged within house churches in order to meet needs and form internal relationships, but the top priority should always be to bring in those who do not know Jesus. This causes the house church to mature and reproduce itself and gives more believers the opportunity to use the gifts the Lord has given to them to reach the lost and make disciples, as well as equipping more people for leadership. Instead of merely watching the functioning of church once a week, each member of the community becomes an active part of the Church, because they work together with the common goal of reaching out to others.

The greatest catalyst for spiritual growth in Christ is turning our eyes from ourselves and setting our sight on Jesus and the needs of those around us. A group of people who are always looking inward and who are content with the status quo will never grow and multiply. When house churches become content to stay the same, they build walls around themselves, causing others to feel unwelcome. On the other hand, the group that has a heart to reach out and to disciple new believers will be willing to change and will enjoy tremendous fellowship and meaningful relationships in the process. All this is to say that an outward focus benefits everyone in the long run, whereas looking inward prevents growth and, like an ingrown toenail, usually causes pain. Looking inward also results in competition and stagnation or, worse, spiritual pride.

We realize that some may disagree with the purpose of the house church, but we believe that we stand on biblical ground when we say that the Church exists to bring glory to God and to introduce people to Jesus. In John 15, Jesus declares to the disciples that they were called to base their lives on the three core values of the Kingdom: to rest daily in the Father's love, to love one another, and to bear witness to Him in the world.

The Great Commission was given to every Christian, not just to the first disciples. When Jesus declared that His disciples are commissioned to go into the world on mission for Him, He did not say that they could vote on whether or not it is a good idea! We, as Jesus' disciples, are sent people. God has one goal: that His own glory would fill the Earth. And God has designed one way to accomplish His goal: through those who know, love and obey His Son, Jesus.

There will be many different creative approaches to reaching the lost and making disciples as we work together in a house-church setting; however, the primary vision must be clear and fixed—we are called to fulfill the Great Commission. Fulfilling the Great Commission requires more than just having weekly evangelistic teachings at our home-church meetings or going out on the street to evangelize. The Great Commission works toward fulfillment when, as individuals in house churches, we reach beyond ourselves to make disciples in our sphere of influence. Through that process, we will discover that God will give us many creative ideas and opportunities. Even if no one immediately comes to Christ through these opportunities, there is a spiritual dynamic released in a community of people that keeps the focus on those who do not know Jesus instead of primarily on individual home-group members. A community of people who have a God-inspired mission and value healthy relationships will be a vibrant community. As we build intentional, authentic relationships, we will impact people's lives.

At the heart of home churches, then, is God's mission. The mission field is the world—the business world, the world of education, the world of arts and entertainment, the worlds of government, science, industry and the marketplace. Some in the Church go to a world of lost people in other nations, and some go to a world of lost people at work or school. Every "world" in which we live and work and play is God's world. When Jesus said that as Christians we are to go into all the world, He meant exactly that. And when He said, "As the Father has sent me, so I also send you," He was absolutely serious.

New Churches Provide More Opportunities to Share Jesus

Dr. C. Peter Wagner, leader of Global Harvest Ministries, has said for years that "the single most effective way to evangelize is to plant new churches."[1]

Fuller Theological Seminary did a research study that found that if a church is 10 or more years old, it takes 85 people to lead 1 person to Christ. If the church is between 4 and 7 years old, it takes 7 people to lead 1 person to Christ. If a church is less than 3 years old, it takes only 3 people to lead 1 person to Christ (see diagram on next page):[2]

Age of Church	People/Salvation Ratio
10+ years old	85:1
4 to 7 years old	7:1
3 years and under	3:1

The results of this study make it abundantly clear: Planting new churches is the most effective way to reach more people. Church planting keeps our faith alive and our focus clear. As micro-churches are planted, we can ask God to reproduce them rapidly within an area. And as the network of these simple churches grows, there will be more and more opportunities to reach people with good news.

Within a network of house churches, some will be more evangelistic than others, depending on the makeup of the persons in the church. This is understandable, but we must not back off from Jesus' command to share His love with those who don't know Him. We are all called to carry our Lord's heart, to reach those people who have not yet decided to follow Christ. Each micro-church needs to strive toward the goal of Jesus' mandate to seek and save those who are lost.

A great example is a group of house churches in Keswick, Ontario, that consists of mostly new believers. They are bringing many nonbelievers into the "family" thanks to their new expression of a more relaxed church atmosphere. These new Christians bring their non-Christian and Christian friends to house-church meetings, where they simply hang out and talk about life and how the Bible applies to everyday situations. These people, and so many others, want spirituality made real. They want *talk* translated into *action*. House churches provide that place of interaction and authenticity.

As the house churches in Ontario prove, it doesn't take long-time believers to affect others for Christ. Some argue, though, that when you have a lot of babies, you will have a lot of messes. When people come to Christ, things can get messy. While this may be true, usually the messy times are when we all grow spiritually. Bring on the babies in Christ! Proverbs 14:4 tells us, "Where there are no oxen, the manger is empty. But from the strength of an ox comes an abundant harvest." We want the abundant harvest, so we are willing to put up with some messes!

Some people tell us that we don't *need* more churches. Let us show you why we *do*. Here is an example: As I (Larry) mentioned earlier, I live in the historically religious community of Lancaster County, Pennsylvania, where there are currently more than 600 churches. That's a lot of churches! However, when you consider the county's population, the current church attendance at each of these churches shows that only 17 percent of the people in our county are involved in the local church.

If 800 new house churches consisting of 25 people each were started this year in our county, the Church would still only be reaching 21.5 percent of the population. This puts things in perspective. We need more community churches, more mega-churches and more house churches networking together to reach those without Christ!

Although for years we have been told that, on average, 40 percent of Americans attend church on a regular basis, we disagree. The picture of what is happening in Lancaster County, Pennsylvania, is true of church attendance all across our nation. Recent studies show the following:

While the U.S. population grew by 13.2 percent from 1900 to 2000 . . . total church attendance grew by only 3 percent. From 2000 to 2004, the U.S. population growth grew by a slightly slower rate—4 percent—while church attendance growth grew by 0.8 percent. By 2020, only about 14 percent of Americans will go to church. By 2050, the figure will drop to less than 10 percent.[3]

America is rapidly becoming a post-Christian nation. We need to wake up and re-evangelize our own country.

What is the best way to re-evangelize? We need new expressions of church that are relevant and close to people's everyday lives. Though some people will only go to a large, impersonal meeting to learn more about following Jesus, we believe that the vast majority of Americans will come to faith in Christ through personal relationships with people who follow Him. We also believe that small, simple, non-building-oriented, non-professional-led, family-based communities are some of the keys for re-evangelizing our nation.

In a recent conversation with a mega-church pastor, I (Floyd) expressed that while mega-churches were growing in number and influence in America, the result was deceptive, because overall we were losing ground. The pastor wouldn't believe me.

There is a false impression that because mega-churches are growing, the Church is growing. The truth is that a smaller and smaller percentage of Americans are willing to attend large, impersonal church meetings. They are searching for more. While mega-churches are growing, the overall numbers of churches and followers of Christ are decreasing in America.

Healthy House Churches Rapidly Reproduce

House-church networks reproduce churches rapidly because the micro-church model lends itself to more authentic relational connections, deeper and more natural discipleship accountability, quick reproduction of leaders and every-member involvement.

According to David Garrison in his book *Church Planting Movements:*

> Church planters often speak of church planting in birthing terms, asking, "How long does it take to birth a new church?" This gestation period varies around the world, just as it does within the animal kingdom. Elephants typically require 22 months to produce an offspring, while rabbits can yield a new litter every three months. Church Planting Movements reproduce like rabbits![4]

It is not hard to see that the numerical potential of micro-churches is enormous.

In Restricted Areas, Churches Meet in Homes

In many cities in America, the construction of church buildings is no longer allowed within the city limits because of zoning restrictions. Exploding urban populations prohibit obtaining real estate to build a church structure. House churches are an obvious solution to this dilemma. Instead of fighting city hall, maybe we should seize the opportunity to multiply multiple numbers of small, simple church communities.

In some parts of the world, house churches start as a matter of necessity, born out of other kinds of legal bans. In my book *House to House,*[5] I (Larry) tell the story of a church in Ethiopia that was forced underground. In 1982, half of all the evangelical churches in Ethiopia were closed due to harassment, legal banning and persecution. The Meserete Kristos Church, for example, fell under a complete ban—all of their church buildings were seized and used for other purposes, and several of their prominent leaders were imprisoned for years without trial or charges.

The Meserete Kristos Church membership at that time was approximately 5,000. As the fires of persecution got hotter and hotter each year, they were forced to meet in clandestine home groups. Nearly a decade later, the Marxist government fell and the same government leaders who closed the doors of the church buildings in the early 1980s led the procession of God's people back into those buildings. The most startling news was that the church had grown while "underground" from 5,000 to more than 50,000 people!

During persecution, these believers met from house to house in small groups. Hundreds of believers began to get involved in the work of ministry in these small house churches. They no longer focused on the church building or church programs. Instead, their time together was spent in prayer and making disciples, reaching those who did not yet know Jesus.

As evident in the Ethiopian church of the late twentieth century, God's agenda for the building of His kingdom includes outreach and discipleship. He wants laborers who are trained to bring in the full harvest: "My food," said Jesus, "is to do the will of him who sent me and to finish his work. Do you not say, 'Four months more and then the harvest'? I tell you, open your eyes and look at the fields! They are ripe for harvest" (John 4:34-36).

Learning from History—The Methodist Revival

We can learn from historical accounts that small groups have often served to fan revival throughout Church history. John Wesley, the founder of the Methodist Church, for example, understood Jesus' concept of putting new wine into new wineskins. He started class meetings to disciple the new believers who were coming to Christ during the Methodist revival in eighteenth-century England. A key to the revival was the accountability that the believers found in the small groups:

> The classes were in effect house churches . . . meeting in
> various neighborhoods where people lived. The class
> leaders (men and women) were disciplers. The classes
> normally met one evening each week for an hour or so.
> Each person reported on his or her spiritual progress, or
> on particular needs or problems, and received the sup-
> port and prayers of the others . . . The class meeting sys-
> tem tied together the widely scattered Methodist people
> and became the sustainer of the Methodist renewal over
> many decades. Now here is the remarkable thing. One
> hears today that it is hard to find enough leaders for
> small groups or for those to carry on the other respon-
> sibilities in the church. Wesley put one in ten, perhaps
> one in five, to work in significant ministry and leader-
> ship. And who were these people? Not the educated or
> the wealthy with time on their hands, but laboring men
> and women, husbands and wives and young folks with
> little or no training, but with spiritual gifts and eager-
> ness to serve . . . Not only did Wesley reach the masses;
> he made leaders of thousands of them.[6]

Gradually, however, the Methodist believers put more emphasis on the weekly church meetings in their buildings. As they
de-emphasized the accountability relationships they had in
their class meetings, the revival movement began to decline.

Peter Bunton, in his book *Cell Groups and House Churches:
What History Teaches Us,* studies a number of examples of house-
church meetings in history. For example, Martin Bucer, a key
figure in the sixteenth-century Reformation, advocated a radical church reformation, which was to begin in small groups or
Christian communities:

Indeed he taught that partaking in such little communities modeled on the New Testament was the only way to keep the Ten Commandments. Additionally, what is of interest is that each group remained connected to others. The leaders were to meet each week, and every one to two months there should be a meeting of all groups in the parish for teaching. (This has some semblance of the structure that Wesley was to establish some two hundred years later.)[7]

Down through history, many movements have emerged to bring the Church back to the way it was in the first century. The house-church vision is a radical reformation of church structure that fits the New Testament configuration of believers meeting in homes.

The Early Church started to erect their own buildings more than 250 years after their beginnings. For centuries, believers met in church buildings for the greater part of their church experience. The modern-day Church has become accustomed to Christians gathering in a church building every Sunday, and it is hard to break that mold. In fact, this form of tradition for tradition's sake gets us into trouble, because we begin to trust a method rather than trusting God for fresh expressions of church that engage our culture and touch our friends' and neighbors' lives. Any church structure, including house churches, can become legalistic and traditional when those who attend trust the method or structure rather than staying flexible and open to God's leading.

House-Church Networks and Missions

Western missionaries have had a tendency to export the only type of wineskin they have experienced—the community church or the mega-church. On the other hand, missionaries who are sent out of house-church networks or from outward-focused cell-based churches project the basic Christian community and New Testament house-church life that they have experienced. Since house-church networks follow the simple pattern in the book of Acts, they can work in any nation or culture. Whereas missionaries from larger-program and building-based churches need to unlearn much of what they have experienced in order to effectively minister the gospel in unreached areas, missionaries with house-church backgrounds don't need to reverse their education.

Much of the training that I (Floyd) do in preparing cross-cultural church planters is to help them unlearn unhelpful and irrelevant models of church that do not fit the needs or cultures of the 3.1 billion people on our planet who have never heard of Jesus. As I lead people through six months of intensive training and coaching to launch their church planting efforts, I find that much of what I do is to help them step away from Western models of church that focus on buildings, programs and educational theories. In my experience, Western church models are unhelpful in most situations and downright harmful in a few situations.[8]

Although our experience has been mostly with small groups in mega-churches and community churches, DOVE Christian Fellowship International, the network of churches that a team of leaders and I (Larry) oversee, has broadened its vision in the last six years to include house-church networks. In light of this change, we have added special training for house-church planters in our current yearly Church Planting and Leadership School. Students from many different movements and denominations come to Pennsylvania one weekend each month for nine months of networking and training on church planting and leadership.[9]

The Mission of God Through House Churches

Jim is an American working in the marketplace who recently realized that he could accomplish the mission of God at his workplace. "I get it now," he said. "I'm a carpenter, but my primary calling is to represent Jesus. I look at the people around me and at the work I do and realize that I am there because I am on a mission for God. I live purposely and have a sense of calling on my life. Every day I wake up and say, 'What assignment do you have for me today, Lord?' "

One of the beauties of house churches is that they catch a sense of destiny from their involvement in simple church communities. House-church members ask, "What's my part? What's my part in reaching people for Jesus? Why has God placed me here? What is God up to and how do I work with God?" They realize they have been called. They are God's people, invading His world and joining His mission for His glory.

On a visit to central India several years ago, I (Floyd) spent time with about a hundred rural house-church leaders. They led small, simple village churches, none larger than 20 or 30 people. As they listened to the reports their coworkers shared about what God was doing in neighboring villages, and as I told stories from Central Asia and China and other parts of the world, they became animated. When I asked one of the senior leaders why this touched them so deeply, he responded, "It gives them dignity and hope. They feel they are part of something big and important." Indeed they are! If only we in the West could get our hope and significance from being part of the big thing God is doing in the world—and not from clothes, possessions, status and other worldly things.

Whatever we do as Christians is for God's glory. The focus of everything we do should be for God. It's important to remember that even church is not for us—it's for God! He did not lead

us to Himself for our glory, but for His. When we believe this
with all our hearts, it will give us the same sense of hope and significance as our brothers and sisters in India.

You've probably noticed that there is one main character in
the Bible—God! The Bible is God's story. Yet, often when we read
the Bible, we read it as if it were about *us*. We look for verses con-
taining encouragement and guidance for *us*. Romans 15:7 tells us
that the goal of all we do is for God to be glorified. God's great
longing is to fill the earth with His glory. He wants to impact and
impress all of Creation with His goodness and greatness.

God longs to accomplish His mission through His people in
the world. If the starting point of all we do is not right, everything
else will be out of alignment. If we get off track right from the
beginning, we will miss our destiny down the road. God must be
the goal of everything—the focus, the reason, the aim—of everything we do. God has a mission and He wants everyone to be a part
of it. The mission is to glorify Himself through His great mercy.

When we are made right in God's eyes, we are saved for God
and called to join Him in spreading the good news of His love
and mercy. The new covenant, the covenant of mercy and grace
that has brought us into relationship with God, is first of all for
God. We are saved for God first, then ourselves.

If the focus and goal of God's plan for all eternity is His own
glory, then we are called to seek, savor and spread His glory. The
Church is not divided into the called and the uncalled, those
who go and those who stay, those who live for His glory and
those who don't. We are on a mission for God—not a secret mission, but an all-consuming mission, and that mission is the
glory of God.

A Christian engineer is to be just as intentional in fulfilling
his mission on the job as is a missionary in Thailand. We are all
called to belong to Jesus. We are called with passions and vocations. There is no unholy place and no unholy vocation to God.

As a church planter in the red-light district of Amsterdam, a mentor once said to me, "Floyd, I want to tell you that the red-light district is a holy place." Well, you can be sure *I* had not thought of it that way! He continued, "The Bible says the whole earth is the Lord's. That means the devil is a squatter here in the red-light district."

If that is true—that the whole earth is the Lord's and that He has designed different dimensions of life involving commerce, education, government and the arts—if He created those spheres of life and put aspirations in us to work and serve in those particular arenas, then what we call "vocations" are *holy callings*. This means that God, by His divine plan, places burdens and desires and abilities and passions in each of us. In doing so, He distributes different aspects of His nature and character in His people. It is God, by His Spirit, who urges us to live for His glory in the different vocations of life. It is God who seeks to mobilize His people who are to live intentionally for His mission and glory.

Joining the Mission of God

When we moved years back to a new neighborhood in Kansas City—a neighborhood of 39 homes— Sally and I (Floyd) believed that we didn't just buy a house we liked; God sent us there to reach our new neighbors for Christ. At the first homeowners meeting we attended, we were appalled by the hostility among our neighbors. The meeting included threats of suing and people shouting obscenities at each other—and gossiping campaigns ran rampant.

Although I was pastoring a community church at the time, our neighborhood was *also* a place God had sent us to do church for Him. As His church in that place, we joined God's mission in prayer for our neighbors. We conducted regular prayer walks around the neighborhood. The more problems there were, the more we prayed. I'd go from house to house late at night and stand in front of our neighbors' homes and say, "God, I invite you into this home. I give you a personal invitation to interrupt their lives." I prayed blessings over them. I prayed for their marriages, their kids and their jobs.

We targeted one lady in particular who just loved to fight and stir up trouble in the neighborhood. After one particularly bad episode, Sally and I bought her a bouquet of flowers and asked to take her and her husband out for dinner. On Mother's Day and other holidays, we gave her gifts and thanked her for her positive contributions to our neighborhood. Although it was a stretch to find them, there were a few positive things she did for the neighborhood.

Through these simple acts of hospitality and prayer, we joined God's mission in our neighborhood. His mission does not have to be pumped up or hyped. We don't have to start it or defend it. God owns His mission, and He will do His mission through us if we allow Him.

Notes

1. Peter Wagner, *Church Planting for a Greater Harvest* (Ventura, CA: Regal Books, 1990), p. 11.
2. "Enlarging Our Borders," American Society for Church Growth (ASCG), report presented to the Executive Presbytery, January 1999.
3. Dave Olson, "Empty Pews, Signs of Hope," *The Covenant Companion*, February 2006, p. 11. http://www.covchurch.org/uploads/mR/5V/mR5VwQf_FolOjJE2DKfOJg/0602FutureorFad.pdf (accessed December 2006).
4. David Garrison, *Church Planting Movements* (Bangalore, India: WIGTake Resources, 2004), p. 194.
5. Larry Kreider, *House to House* (Lititz, PA: House to House Publications, 1995), p. 102.
6. Howard A. Snyder, *The Radical Wesley* (Downers Grove, IL: InterVarsity Press, 1996), pp. 53-57, 63.
7. Peter Bunton, *Cell Groups and House Churches: What History Teaches Us* (Lititz, PA: House to House Publications, 2001), p. 14.
8. See Floyd's personal website: www.floydandsally.com for more about how he trains church planters, or write to Floyd at floyd.mcclung@gmail.com for more information.
9. See DOVE Christian Fellowship International's many training options under "Training Schools" at www.dcfi.org.

CHAPTER 4

THE ROLE OF SPIRITUAL FATHERS AND MOTHERS

If doing church in a house church were simply another layer of meetings to add to our already busy lives, it would wear us out and quickly lose its appeal. Fortunately, doing church with a small group of friends is *not* another set of meetings, but a community of people we become a part of. It is a spiritual family. A major aspect of house-church community as family is *spiritual parenting*—when spiritual fathers and mothers release themselves to be reproduced in others.

I (Larry) will never forget the experience of having our first baby. I had faithfully attended prenatal classes with LaVerne, where I learned how to coach her through her labor. But when the contractions started, it hit me: We were going to have a baby! I didn't feel like I was ready. I was too young. We had never done this before. I felt like telling LaVerne, "Couldn't you just put it on hold for a few months until we are ready?" But waiting was not an option. She was going to give birth, and our baby girl was to be born whether I felt ready or not.

It really felt strange to be a papa. Though we had never been down the parenting road before, with the faithful advice of trusted family and friends, somehow it all worked out.

That was more than 30 years ago. When this "baby" girl got married, we gave her away. She had gone from being a baby to a teenager and then to an adult, and was then ready to parent the next generation. As of this writing, she has given birth to three children, and these grandchildren of mine will go on to be parents themselves when another generation is born!

When it comes to spiritual parenting, many potential spiritual parents go through the same emotions that physical parents do: "How could God ever use me to be a spiritual parent? What if I can't do it properly? Am I really ready for this?" However, as they are encouraged to take a step of faith and obedience, they begin to experience the joy of becoming a spiritual father or mother. They have the satisfaction of training and releasing others for eternity.

Just as healthy biological parents expect their children to leave home and start their own families, healthy spiritual parents must think the same way. Christian leaders, especially house-church leaders, are also called to "give away" the believers they serve so that they may start their own spiritual families—new house churches.

According to the Bible, there are three different types of people in our churches: spiritual children, young men and women, and fathers and mothers. First John 2:12-13 tells us:

> I write to you, dear children, because your sins have been forgiven on account of his name. I write to you, fathers, because you have known him who is from the beginning. I write to you, young men, because you have overcome the evil one.

Let's take a look at these three types of people and how they can be prepared and trained to become spiritual parents.

1. Spiritual Children

The Church is filled with spiritual orphans. There are many believers in the Church who have never been fathered or mothered. The root of the problem seems to be that many "baby Christians" have never grown up—many are even unaware that they are still infants in Christ. Their *chronological* spiritual age may be 20, 30, 40 or 50 years, but they remain "on the milk." They make a fuss when they don't get their own way, complain about not being fed, and have not yet taken spiritual responsibility to reach and train others to know, love and obey Jesus.

2. Spiritual Young Men and Women

Spiritual young men, according to the Bible, have the Word of God abiding in them and have overcome the wicked one. They have learned to feed on the Word for themselves in order to overcome the devil, but they have not yet become spiritual fathers.

When we were children, we thought our fathers knew everything. Then we grew into adolescence and discovered there were a few things Dad didn't know. By the time we were in our mid-teens, in our youthful arrogance, we figured that our fathers were still living in the stone age. But when we became parents, we were shocked at how much our dads had learned since we were teenagers! In reality, by becoming a parent ourselves, our perspective changed. Having spiritual children also changes our perspective.

When we have spiritual children, we become more aware of our own need to learn from others. We want spiritual moms and dads to mentor and coach us. We want to follow God's will in our own lives, but we don't want to do it without godly input from those who are older than us in the Lord.

3. Spiritual Fathers and Mothers

One of the greatest catalysts to maturity as a Christian is to become a spiritual father or mother. Many of the problems that surface in churches today are the product of (1) spiritual young men and women who are full of the Word of God but have not had the experience of becoming spiritual parents, and (2) church leaders who have not trained, modeled and released the young men and women within their church to have their own spiritual children. House churches can solve these training and leadership issues if home-church members and leaders develop spiritual fathers and mothers in-house in a natural, family-like setting.

How Do We Become Spiritual Parents?

The apostle Paul told the Corinthian church that they desperately needed fathers:

> Even though you have ten thousand guardians in Christ, you do not have many fathers; for in Christ Jesus I became your father through the gospel. Therefore I urge you, to imitate me (1 Cor. 4:15-16).

So, how does a young man or woman become a spiritual parent? The only way for a young man or woman to become a spiritual parent is to have children, either by adoption (becoming a spiritual father or mother to someone who is already a believer but needs to be discipled) or by natural birth (becoming a spiritual father or mother to someone you have personally led to Christ, and committing yourself to helping that person grow). Paul became a spiritual father to Onesimus through "natural birth," leading him to Christ in prison (see Philem. 10). Paul also became a spiritual father to Timothy, only this time through "adoption," after meeting him in Ephesus (see Acts 16:1-4).

House churches and cell groups provide an ideal opportunity for everyone to experience life as part of a spiritual family and eventually become spiritual parents. The purpose for house-church multiplication and cell multiplication is to create opportunities for everyone in the group to have the joy of leading their friends to Christ and then helping them grow spiritually.

A Spiritual Father Defined

Scripture warns us about giving ourselves an impressive title in an effort to gain the honor and respect of others: "Do not call anyone on earth your father; for One is your Father, He who is in heaven . . . But he who is greatest among you shall be your servant" (Matt. 23:9,11, *NKJV*). A spiritual father is always a servant first. No one can ever take the place of our heavenly Father—spiritual fathers are responsible for pointing their spiritual children to their heavenly Father.

The apostle Paul called himself a father several times in Scripture but used the word "father" to denote "not *authority*, but *affection*: therefore he calls them not his *obliged*, but his *beloved*, sons" (see 1 Cor. 4:14).[1] A spiritual father's measure of greatness is his level of servanthood and love, not his position.

Spiritual fathers and mothers could also be called "mentors." A spiritual mentor recognizes that people need to be developed through a caring and empathetic coaching approach, which models and explains to them how to grow in Christ. Simply stated, our favorite definition of a spiritual parent is this: *A spiritual father or mother helps a spiritual son or daughter reach his or her God-given potential.* Spiritual parenting is uncomplicated and deeply profound. Bobb Biehl says it this way: "Mentoring is more 'How can I help you?' than 'What should I teach you?'"[2]

Floyd and I (Larry), along with our wives, have both had the joy of pouring our lives into young men and women we connected with many years ago. More than 30 years ago, LaVerne and I and a team of young people began to develop Paul-Timothy relationships with new Christians. I met with a few young men each week for Bible study and prayer and tried to answer their questions about life. LaVerne did the same with young women. Watching them grow from spiritual babies into young men and women and then into spiritual parents themselves has brought great joy to our lives. It has also caused great growth in our own spiritual lives.

Sally and I (Floyd) did the same thing while living on two houseboats in the main harbor of Amsterdam, Holland. Recently, I conducted a workshop for the leaders of missional communities in Germany. One of the leaders in attendance was a single woman named Christine, from Stuttgart. Christine was the leader of a unique outreach community called the JezusFreaks. She told me, "You are my spiritual grandfather. Some of the people you led to Christ in Amsterdam came to Germany to share Jesus with their friends, and as a result, I became a follower of Jesus." She spoke with affection and a radiant smile. It was a sweet experience for me—one that makes all the hardships of vocational ministry worthwhile!

Reproducing Ourselves

The heart of what we do, as mature fathers and mothers, is to reproduce ourselves in others. Our Father in Heaven wants us to have the experience of raising up sons and daughters, just as He has done with us—His children. However, we cannot take part in spiritual parenting without being personally involved in the lives of people who don't know Jesus.

As we share Jesus with others and encourage them to grow in their new faith in Him, it is only natural that they, in turn, will want to tell others about what has happened to them. As they do, we can mentor them through the process of delivering the message of Jesus as they gather their friends around meals and times of hanging out together. In this natural way, new communities begin.

My (Larry) extended family gathers every year for a reunion— aunts, uncles, brothers, sisters, cousins, nephews and nieces, all connected to the Kreider family. When my grandparents were alive, I noticed how they seemed to look at each other with a twinkle in their eyes at these family gatherings. They knew we were all there because of them, and it gave them deep satisfaction to see their posterity.

Likewise, the Lord wants to see spiritual families continually reproducing in each generation. He has a generational perspective that stretches beyond my grandparents' scope, and we must develop such a perspective, too. In the Old Testament, God is called "the God of Abraham, Isaac and Jacob"—even His very name shows a generational connection!

God has an inheritance for each one of us—a posterity of spiritual descendants who carry on the spiritual DNA that has been passed down from one generation to another. One way to claim your spiritual inheritance is to gather your spiritual children and build a community with them—a simple, small, life-giving community. This community is a spiritual family. Communities formed by spiritual families are the heart of a healthy, relationship-based house church. Know who your spiritual sons and daughters are and invest wisely and faithfully in their lives.

Our Inheritance: Spiritual Children

This promise of spiritual children is for every Christian! God has placed us here on Earth because He has called us to become spiritual fathers and mothers to others. Along with this responsibility comes the expectation that our spiritual children will have spiritual children of their own who will continue to produce more children after them.

Our inheritance for eternity will be the spiritual children that we can some day present to Jesus Christ. No matter what we do—whether we are a homemaker, a student, a factory worker, a pastor of a church, or the head of a large corporation—we have the divine blessing and responsibility to birth spiritual children who will produce grandchildren and great grandchildren.

Each of us is called to impart to others the rich inheritance that God has given us.

I (Floyd) can remember praying as a young man that just as my grandparents and parents served the Lord, so I would continue the covenant He had made with them. I also made a covenant with God in which I requested that He would do the same thing He was doing through me, spiritually, through my children and spiritual children.

It was God's promise—to fulfill an as-yet-unfulfilled inheritance of spiritual sons and daughters—that led Sally and me to move to South Africa. We were 60 and 57 years of age when we said yes to God. We heard God promise us an inheritance on the continent of Africa, and particularly in South Africa, which led us to say yes to His call to move to Cape Town in the autumn of 2006. We have been in Cape Town since then, equipping leaders and reaching people with the good news, while God's promise remains in our hearts.

How did Abraham respond when the Lord showed him the stars in the sky and promised him descendants just as numerous? The Bible says, "Abram believed the Lord" (Gen. 15:6). What did he believe the Lord for? His inheritance! We, too, need to "believe the Lord" in order to gain many spiritual children.

We can trust God to reap the harvest and bring His children home to Him. It may not happen overnight, but it will happen when we trust in God's faithfulness and we get involved—both with those who don't know Jesus and with those we can mentor. We are *promised* an inheritance of spiritual children. God *wants* to give us an inheritance of spiritual children, and He *will* do it if we do our part.

Healthy Families Multiply

We can only take two things with us to heaven: ourselves and our spiritual sons and daughters. You will never be sorry if you devote yourself to investing in others. They will be the reward you present to Jesus when you bow before Him—think of the joy

He will have over your obedience to be a faithful mother or father to those He gave to you! And His reward, His joy over having the love and worship of those you brought to Him, will be your reward as well.

In the Bible, we see Paul's longing to visit his spiritual children in Thessalonica. He says in 1 Thessalonians 2:19-20, "For what is our hope, our joy or the crown in which we will glory in the presence of our Lord Jesus when he comes? Is it not you? Indeed, you are our glory and joy." His spiritual children were his glory and joy—his inheritance! Paul rejoiced like a winner receiving a garland of victory (crown) at the Olympic games when he thought of his spiritual children and grandchildren whom he would present to Christ.

A Spiritual Legacy

I (Larry) mention in my book *The Cry for Spiritual Fathers and Mothers* that a few years ago, I was in Barbados training church leaders and believers on the subject of spiritual parenting and small-group ministry. The day I was to leave to come back to the U.S., Bill Land—a missionary who leads Youth With A Mission's Caribbean ministry—asked me to his home. Bill and his family, along with a team of leaders, spend their time training and equipping Christians to become spiritual leaders in the Caribbean. On this visit to Barbados, Bill told me some interesting history about this tiny island nation.

He explained that many in Barbados came as slaves to the island years ago from West Africa, including the nation of Gambia. Now, after receiving Christ and being trained as missionaries, Barbadians were being sent to their ancestral country of Gambia to lead Muslim Gambians to Christ. With a common heritage, it was the ideal match. While explaining this, Bill said something that moved me deeply, "Larry, do you realize the people being reached in Gambia are a part of your spiritual heritage? You were one of my spiritual fathers."[3]

As I sat on the plane, returning to the United States, I was dumbfounded over Bill's words. More than 20 years ago, long before I was a pastor or a writer or a church leader, I was a young chicken farmer who led a Bible study of young people. During that time, I became one of Bill's spiritual fathers. Bill in turn became a spiritual father to those he discipled in Barbados, and the Barbadian Christians who were now going to Africa and leading Gambians to Christ were my spiritual great-grandchildren! Generations to come would receive God's promises because a chicken farmer had been obedient to God's call to disciple a bunch of teenagers. Yes, this was part of my spiritual legacy. As I pondered this reality, I was deeply moved by the Lord. I had, indeed, become the recipient of a large inheritance!

God has called each one of us to be spiritual parents. The Lord wants to give us a spiritual legacy. We may not feel ready; in fact, we may feel unprepared. Nevertheless, God's call remains on our lives.

Restoring the New Testament Pattern

Although for the past 1,700 years much of the Church has strayed from relational restoration between fathers and sons and mothers and daughters, we sense that the Lord is breathing a fresh infusion of the truth about relationships to people all over the world. There is an unprecedented number of men and women who are investing their lives in spiritual sons and daughters. Rather than focusing on meetings and buildings, which promote *programs* to encourage the spiritual growth of believers, these moms and dads in the Lord are relationally imparting to others what the Father has given to them. They are responding to God's call to be His *family* as they return to the New Testament principle of building spiritual families. Many believers are meeting house to house in small groups throughout the world because the Lord is restoring this sense of spiritual family to the Body of Christ. Some prefer to call it community. Whatever you call it, we believe the heart of what is happening is the Lord's restoration of spiritual family. Christians are beginning to relive the book of Acts. They are seeing the importance of empowering and parenting the next generation, which is crying out for faith mentors.

Jesus wants His Church to be restored to the New Testament pattern of family life. He ministered to the multitudes but focused on a few (the disciples). These few changed the world—and we can do the same!

Thirsting for New Wine

We are convinced that the Lord is preparing to pour out His Spirit and bring revival to the Church in these last days—not a sit-in-meetings-and-keep-it-to-yourself type of revival, but a go-to-the-streets revival like we read about in the book of Acts; not a sit-and-wait-for-God-to-do-something revival, but an obey-the-Great-Commission-and-do-what-God-has-commanded-us-to-do type of revival. Already, more people have come to Christ in the last half-century than during any other time in the history of the Church. Consider China, where there are close to 100 million Christians, and South Korea, which changed from a Buddhist nation to one in which one-third of the population professes Jesus Christ.

It is our hope and prayer that there will be an even greater awakening to the things of God in our communities, cities and institutions. Instead of a new reformation, we long to see a refor*mission*. When the Lord pours out this new wine, we must have new wineskins prepared, or we could lose the harvest. The wineskins (church structures) of the Early Church were simple in nature: People met from house to house. We believe our Lord's strategy to prepare for the harvest is still the same—He wants ordinary believers who have encountered an extraordinary God to meet together as spiritual families from house to house (and factory to factory, and business to business, and school to school) to disciple and train each other in preparation for the harvest.

Many Christians today are thirsting for this great influx of new wine—new believers pouring into His kingdom. God is placing a desire within spiritual fathers and mothers to welcome these believers into the Kingdom and then to train them as spiritual sons and daughters. Small groups of believers who meet in homes provide an ideal structure for this kind of training.

Structure Without Relationships Equals Boredom

Although house churches and house-church networks are wonderful wineskins for spiritual parenting, house churches in themselves are not the answer. Plainly stated, *it is not the structure that is significant, but the relationships that occur within its perimeters.* If people in house churches do not practice spiritual parenting, their groups may quickly become as boring and as lifeless as any other structure. The life comes from the active father-son and mother-daughter and friend-to-friend relationships that take place within the house-church network.

You Can Be a Spiritual Parent, Too!

Perhaps you feel that you have already tried to be a spiritual parent but have failed. Trust God for grace and start again! Someone once asked Mother Teresa what she did when she got discouraged because she did not see immediate results. "God does not demand that I be successful," she said. "God demands that I be faithful. When facing God, results are not important. Faithfulness is what is important."[4]

Maybe you never had a spiritual father or mother. You can still give someone else what you never had by being his or her spiritual mentor. You do not need to be perfect, just faithful and obedient. Be available to others. Be a servant. Get involved with a ministry or small group in your church, or even join or start a house church. Get to know people. Become the best listener in the group! Pray for people daily. And then watch God turn it on for you! Don't be surprised when people ask if you have time for them. Take the ones that God lays on your heart out for coffee. Ask how they are doing, and listen. Speak words of encouragement. Don't try to fix people—love them! Don't wait until you have taken three years of counseling classes, read 10 books on mentoring and attended unending workshops on discipleship. Start small. Everyone is capable of discipling between one and three people. You cannot wait until you think you are ready to be a perfect disciple-maker, because that will never happen.

If you feel hesitant about mentoring, you are in good company. Moses told the Lord that he couldn't speak properly. Jeremiah said he was too young. Joshua was scared. Gideon thought that he had been brought up in the wrong family.

Even your chronological age is no excuse. You can be a spiritual parent at 18 or 80. A 12-year-old girl in our house group became a spiritual parent to younger kids in the group. She took them under her wing and taught them simple biblical principles from God's Word. She prayed with them and cared for them when they had a need. She learned by *doing*. Out of her love for Jesus and for those kids, she took small steps of obedience. She did not wait until she felt totally equipped; she became a spiritual parent while she was still learning and while she was still a kid herself.

As you involve yourself and invest in others' lives, the very atmosphere of your house church will change. Pray for it, expect it and step out in faith. Keep a servant's heart and a humble spirit, and God will show you those who want to be mentored for growth into spiritual adulthood.

Notes
  1. Bobb Biehl, *Mentoring* (Nashville, TN: Broadman and Holman Publishers, 1996), p. 19.
  2. *Matthew Henry's Commentary in One Volume* (Grand Rapids, MI: Zondervan, 1960), p. 119.
  3. Larry Kreider, *The Cry for Spiritual Fathers and Mothers* (Lititz, PA: House to House Publications, 2000), p. 93.
  4. *Mother Teresa: In My Own Words,* compiled by Jose Luis Gonzalez-Balado (New York: Random House, 1996), p. 40.

CHAPTER 5

OUR MEASURING STICK: THE VIBRANT, EARLY CHURCH MODEL

J esus modeled *church as community*. He defined church in the simplest of terms for the disciples so that they would understand what He had in mind for the new movement He was starting. Church happened for Jesus and the Twelve as they formed a community that learned, lived and served together. The apostle Paul understood and followed Jesus' example of Church as missional community living. It first happened for Paul when he told a women's prayer meeting in Philippi the good news about Jesus, then gathered and taught them in the home of their leader, Lydia. It happens today when a family invites a few friends over for a meal on a regular basis and seeks to grow together as followers of Jesus. When people eat together, they are the church gathered together. When they seek to obey the commands of Jesus together, they are a church with clear purpose. When several like-minded, small communities band together, they become a community network, while growing together in a shared vision. Ideally, such networks meet both in one another's homes to experience depth of friendship and discipleship and in larger celebrations to experience a greater sense of what God is up to in their movement.

In the Early Church, believers opened up their homes to experience the dynamic church life that occurred as thousands of people decided to follow Jesus. In one instance, about 3,000 people were added to the Church during the span of one day! How could a small band of Jesus' followers possibly have taken care of 3,000 new believers? They couldn't. Part of their secret is found in Acts 2:45-47:

> They sold their possessions and shared the proceeds with those in need. They worshiped together at the Temple each day, met in homes for the Lord's Supper, and shared their meals with great joy and generosity—all the while praising God and enjoying the goodwill of all the people. And each day the Lord added to their group (*NLT*).

The Early Christians began to help one another and to explain the good news to those who didn't know about Jesus. Following Jesus, as described in the book of Acts, indicates that the key to keeping house groups healthy is reaching out to others. They were a church for God and others, not a church for themselves.

The Church Met in Homes

When the Church began, it followed Jesus' pattern of reaching out and family life. It says in Acts 2:42 that "They devoted themselves to the apostles' teaching and to the fellowship, to the breaking of bread and to prayer." In Acts 20:20, we read that the apostle Paul does the same thing: "I never shrank from telling you the truth, either publicly or in your homes" (*NLT*).

The letter that Paul wrote to the Christians in Rome was addressed to believers in Jesus Christ who met in people's homes. In his letter to the Romans, Paul indicates that one of these groups met in Priscilla and Aquila's home:

> Greet Priscilla and Aquila, my fellow workers in Christ Jesus. They risked their lives for me. Not only I but all

the churches of the Gentiles are grateful to them. Greet also *the church that meets at their house* (Rom. 16:3-5, emphasis added).

Paul also sent his greetings to the churches that met in the homes of Aristobulus and Narcissus (see Rom. 16:10-11). When Paul wrote to his friend Philemon, he expressed his greetings to the church in his house: "To Philemon our dear friend and fellow worker, to Apphia our sister, to Archippus our fellow soldier and to the church that meets in your home" (Philem. 1:2).

This pattern of meeting in people's homes is duplicated many times in the New Testament. Paul met with the Philippian jailor and his entire family in their home to teach them about Jesus, and as a result they all decided to become followers of Jesus (see Acts 16:30-34). The believers in Philippi met in homes such as Lydia's (see Acts 16:15,40). The church in Colossi met in Nymphas's home (see Col. 4:15). Paul used his own house as a teaching center near the end of his life, when he welcomed all and taught without hindrance from the Roman authorities.

Peter and Mary, John Mark's mother, were also involved in house church. Peter met at Cornelius's house with his family and friends. Mary hosted house-church meetings in her own home. There was a very natural flow of church as these Early Christians lived, shared meals, worked and prayed together (see Acts 10:22-48; 12:12). Church was how they lived, not a place where they attended.

The book of Acts records the birth and spontaneous multiplication of the Church as accomplished through the many early home churches. Interestingly, the story of how the Church was birthed begins and ends in peoples' homes (see Acts 28:30-31).

Radical Change

The Bible defines church very simply because God wants everyone who follows Jesus to be part of it. Jesus came not only to die
on the cross for our sins but also to empower every person who
follows Him to discover their place in His spiritual family, the
Church. That's one of the reasons He made us all "priests" in
the Church.

In Old Testament times, only a few men were chosen to be
a priest. But Jesus changed that arrangement. He taught that
everyone who believed in Him was a priest. What that meant
to the Jewish audience of His day was that everyone had a part
to play, not just a few men. What that means for us today is
that we don't have to go to a Bible school for four years to be
a leader in the Church. In fact, Jesus defined leaders in a new
way—as servants.

When Jesus came, He turned everything on its head. He
made *everyone* who believed in Him a servant-leader: tax collec-
tors, fishermen, political terrorists, Roman officers, and men
and women alike. Everyone was invited to be part of the
Church. This new way of doing things was called the *ecclesia*—a
term familiar to the people of the day. It was a Greek word used
to describe the ordinary people who made up the governing
body of Greek city-states. *Ecclesia* referred to the convened
assembly of all the citizens of a city—and today, that's who we
are as members of the Church. We are the ones who have been
given authority to make things happen. We have been given a
mandate to make decisions, take action and serve others, as
long as we do it in obedience to the commands of Jesus.

One example of the radical change God brought about was
when the Church first came to Europe. It started in the home
of a woman—a businesswoman. Her name was Lydia. Paul
heard about a group of God-fearing women meeting to pray by

the river outside of Philippi. Though women meeting to pray together outside of a religious building is not very remarkable to our Western way of thinking, in the first century this was a radical departure from the temple-centered practices of the Jews and the Greeks. Lydia responded to Paul's preaching with a trusting heart and became the functional leader of the first church that started on the European continent.

If your way of thinking about Church is institutional and doctrinal, you will patronize Lydia's role and minimize it, but if you think of the *ecclesia* as the Bible defines it—as a spiritual family—you will see that God very intentionally used Lydia, a woman, to lead the first church in Europe. A house church that met in Lydia's home was exactly how God wanted it—nothing fancy, just a community of people built around the leadership gifts of a businesswoman who opened her home to Paul and his coworkers (see Acts 16:14-40).

The Modern Church Dilemma

Down through the ages, the Church lost the New Testament component of meeting in small groups and placed more of an emphasis on the Church as it meets in large buildings. This practice started about 300 years after the birth of the Early Church (the Church we read about in the book of Acts), when Constantine built assembly places for the Christians to meet in. During this time, many Christians started meeting in these "church buildings" rather than in people's homes.

We believe that followers of Jesus should get back to seeing the Church as *people*, not as a place where people meet. As a result of depending on buildings and programs rather than community, the contemporary Church, especially in the Western world, is sinking fast. Statistics concerning the contemporary Church are dismal. They show that the Church is losing its relevance in today's diverse and pluralistic world. Let's look at some sobering facts:

- The U.S. ranks third behind China and India in the number of unsaved people. Evangelical churches have failed to gain an additional 2 percent of the American population in the past 50 years. In other words, we are not even reaching our own children.[1]

- Approximately 3,500 to 4,000 churches close their doors for the last time each year, while 1,100 to 1,500 churches are started each year.[2]

- Churches that reach the unchurched are highly intentional, and they understand the culture. A large element of cultural awareness is understanding the generation born between 1977-1994. Research indicates that only 4 percent of this group are Christians. This is the most unchurched generation in America.[3]

Today's Church has tried to reach people for Christ with extravagant church programs and twenty-first-century techniques and methodology. While such methods may have a place, we believe they are overrated and have, in many instances, led to an impersonal and offensive way of doing things—all in the name of God. Technology and programs can never substitute for personal relationships formed in the context of genuine Christian community.

God has created the Church to be a dynamic, growing, relational movement. The Holy Spirit invites every generation and every race of people to create new expressions of Church. Jesus called these new expressions "wineskins." This is part of the adventure of being the Church: The Father takes a lot of joy in allowing us to create new wineskins, i.e., new ways of doing church. He wants us to break out of the old ways to find new ways of doing church, and He wants us, in the process, to discover the power that is latent in the Church as the *ecclesia*—the empowered people of God.

Do Church Like They Did in the Book of Acts

It's time we read the book of Acts with new eyes. We invite you to read it and to dream about what the Church could be today. When we read the book of Acts, we read about a church that shared their possessions with one another. We see, in our mind's eye, a community of people who were generous, vibrant, growing and courageous. It was a community of people who were wildly in love with Jesus, not an institution devoted to buildings and programs. In Acts, we see friends in one another's homes, remembering the Lord's death by celebrating communion as they eat together. We see them worshiping with whatever musical instruments they can find, making joyful sounds as they praise God for sending Jesus. We try to imagine the small communities of Jesus followers spontaneously multiplying all over Jerusalem—the teachers, prophets and evangelists moving between the groups of believers, making sure they stay connected to one another.

The Church in the book of Acts functioned as a vibrant *community*, not a weekly meeting. They were certainly not a megachurch as we understand it today. Instead, they were a dynamic movement of small communities, spontaneously breaking out all over the city. They occasionally met together in big celebrations on the porch of Solomon's temple. They gathered in each other's homes, crowding into living rooms and gardens and workshops—wherever they could find space to gather and worship and pray for their friends and family. They infiltrated every part of the city and every sphere of society.

Think about the power of what was happening: They often spent time fasting, worshiping and speaking words of encouragement to one another. They preached boldly about Jesus. Common people were discovering their abilities to teach, pray for the sick, serve and organize. Everyone was involved, thanks to the simple model of gathering in small communities. The whole Church was actively engaged, not just a few. Their way of life was attractive to those with whom they came in contact— which makes sense, since what the people had known for years was the impersonal and oppressive authority of the Pharisees. God breathed on the dry bones of Judaism, and an army of ordinary people came to life. It was an army of the ordinary called out by the stirring of God in their hearts.

Notes
1. Arden Adamson, "Enlarging Our Borders," Wisconsin-Northern Michigan District, report presented to the Executive Presbytery, January 1999.
2. American Society for Church Growth, "Enlarging Our Borders," report presented to the Executive Presbytery, January 1999.
3. Ibid.

CHAPTER 6

WHAT DOES A HOUSE CHURCH LOOK LIKE?

House church is a model of Church that really excites us. Nevertheless, we are quick to say that no one model of church will reach the whole world. We are not interested in the most recent craze or the newest fad in church structure or method. We've had all kinds of spiritual fads and swings in the Body of Christ, and we do not want to do church that way anymore.

Then why are we involved in house churches? It's not because they are the best thing or the better thing. It's not because they are new or because we're mad at anyone. We believe that one should never build something in a spirit of pride, anger or rebellion.

Simply put, we know that small church communities work, not only because they are biblical, but also because they get people involved, produce accountability and reproduce leaders, along with the added bonus of functioning in close proximity to those who don't know Jesus.

Above all, we believe that house churches bring glory to God.

There are many types of micro-churches springing up throughout North America and in the nations of the world. Whenever we feel that we have the perfect model, the Lord will stretch us by giving someone in our church or community a new vision that will force us to think outside of the box.

Certainly, we cannot put God in a box!

House churches are flexible and fluid and can take place in any location. Church can be as simple as gathering around a meal in a café, to meeting in a business boardroom, to laughing and fellowshipping together in a park, a mall, art gallery, factory or youth center. The time together should regularly include breaking bread and remembering the Lord's death and resurrection, preferably around meals and times of fellowship; singing; praying for those in need; and giving to each other and to the outreach of the corporate body as it reaches out to others. What you do can be as practical as asking the Lord, "How can we reach out to our friends and neighbors together?" and then obeying what He tells you to do.

What Is the Church?

Before talking more about house churches and what they look like, perhaps we should pause for a moment and make sure we have a clear understanding of the nature of church.

What is the Church, exactly? The Church is not a building or a meeting or a program. The Church of Jesus Christ is simply *people*. As believers, we are the Church. Since the word "church"— *ekklesia* in Greek—literally means *called out ones,* the Church is a group of people who have been called from spiritual darkness into the light and called to obey the Great Commission.

The Universal Church

When we come to Christ, we are immediately a part of the universal Church of Christ, which includes every believer from any nation of the world. Everywhere we travel throughout the world, we find believers from completely different backgrounds, with different skin colors and different cultures, but who have one thing in common: They all have the same heavenly Father. They have received Jesus Christ as Lord and are part of the same family.

Once while flying in an airplane, a businessman sitting next to me (Larry) began to tell me about the corporation he represented. Then he asked me, "What do you do?" I told him that I was a part of the largest corporation in the world. "In fact," I said, "we are now in every country of the world." Of course, I was talking about the Church—God's wonderful and universal family, the Church of Jesus Christ.

The Bible is talking about the universal Church when it says that all the saints of the whole Church of God and all His children in heaven and on Earth will acknowledge that Jesus Christ is alone worthy: "With your blood you purchased men for God from every tribe and language and people and nation" (Rev. 5:9).

The Local Church

The word "church" also refers to the *local* church. Within God's universal Church family are *local* churches of many sizes, types and styles. In each community, these churches provide the support and love each believer needs.

According to Joel Comiskey, author, speaker and church planter in southern California, a New Testament local church must be under the Lordship of Christ, be mutually accountable to other local churches, participate in the sacraments, and have regular meetings under God-ordained leadership:

> The many references to the New Testament local house church indicate that it physically met at a certain time and at a certain place. Taken together with the leadership emphasis, I think a local church should have regular meetings under God ordained leadership. I say this in opposition to the idea that a local church might simply be believers meeting "once in a while" at Starbucks or a Chris Tomlin concert.[1]

A true local church then, as we understand it, is a group of believers who are committed to the Lord and to one another, committed to obeying His Word, committed to a common vision, and accountable to spiritual leadership. They are a group of believers meeting together regularly, caring for one another, watching out for one another and corporately seeking to worship, serve God and reach those who do not know Jesus. That is a local church, whatever its size, style or building in which it meets. Simple!

House Churches Are Real Churches

House churches are not mere appendages of the larger Church. They are real churches, according to David Garrison in *Church Planting Movements*:

> House churches are stand-alone churches that happen to be small enough to meet in homes. After filling their limited space, they grow through multiplication rather than increasing their membership. Each house church has its own leadership and derives its authority directly from Christ, rather than through a church hierarchy, and functions in every way as a church.[2]

Each house church is a fully functioning church in itself. It has leaders who facilitate the involvement of everyone in the group. Meetings are participatory and interactive family-type gatherings where everyone has the opportunity to contribute something. Participants gather weekly to explore issues of faith or work on projects as they study the Bible, eat, pray, play, share the Lord's Supper and baptize new believers.

These micro-churches are led by average folk who love Christ and other people. They have discovered that life is about loving

God and connecting with others as they strive to become more like Christ. People can't hide in a small community. In a house church, as in any other healthy small group, participants learn to be transparent as they interact and are accountable to one another.

Rad Zdero, who started a movement of house churches in Canada, aptly describes what those in micro-churches are looking for:

> These folks simply want to rediscover the power and person of Jesus in community and as they engaged in mission, as his early followers did. No church buildings, professional clergy, highly polished services, or expensive programs are required or desired.[3]

Zdero says that people are attracted to home churches because they allow people to explore their faith on their own initiative with people who share their views.

House churches are people loving people. This point was made real to me (Floyd) when a family lost their one-week-old son, Isaac. The first time I saw the parents after returning from a trip was at the graveside service. Though the sadness was palpable, one message came through loud and clear: Ray and Maxine Nelson and their little daughter, Briana, had been surrounded by friends who loved them. They sat with them at the hospital, brought them meals and cried with them in their pain and confusion.

I thought afterward, *What would the Nelsons have done without a community of friends to love them through this painful time? How hard would it have been for them without friends to share their sorrows and help them move forward after family and relatives went back home?* God shows His love and cares for His people through other people. Thus, a house church reveals the love of God when we stand with each other, especially when there are no pat answers or easy solutions.

House Churches Engage Communities with Jesus

As a teenager, I (Floyd) was urged to "bring your friends to church."
I tried that a few times. It was a bitter disaster. I brought one of
my best friends with me to church—a guy named Gary. Gary was
a tall basketball player like me. We hung out a lot, studied
together and were both too shy to date—so we ate, drank and
slept basketball. That was basically our life! After a lot of plead-
ing on my part, Gary finally gave in and attended one of our
church meetings. The service was great as far as Pentecostal services go. People danced in the aisles, shouted, clapped their hands
and worshiped God joyfully—but it freaked Gary out. For someone like Gary, with very little church background, it was too
much. Luckily our friendship survived "the meeting." He still
hung out with me, but he thought I was a little weird after that.

By the time I went away to university, I was totally put off
by church. I was tired of meetings—especially super-sized, over-
the-top worship and preachers who screamed at people instead
of talking to them from the heart. I got to the place where I
could spot a phony a mile away. Fortunately, I met some guys
in my dorm at university who genuinely loved Jesus. Church for
me became late night prayer meetings with my friends, early
morning devotions with one of the guys, and weekly worship
times with the guys in the residence hall.

I continued on to a good experience of church in Afghanistan. I didn't go there to find church—you could say it found me.
My wife and I rented a big house in Kabul and opened our home
to anyone in need. We were there to help foreigners, people who
got sick, who lost their passports or got strung out on drugs. We
ran a free clinic and teahouse downtown and took in the homeless and drugged-out "world travelers." Kabul, Afghanistan, was
not a good place to get sick—you could catch more diseases in
the local hospital than you came in with. Soon we had 20 to 30

people living with us at a time. We rented more houses to take everyone in. Hundreds of young world travelers became followers of Jesus over the few years we lived in Afghanistan.

As I look back on our time there, I can see how we emphasized belonging more than believing. We shared our meals together, played soccer together and developed a routine of prayer and Bible study before we did work projects or visited people in the prisons and hospitals. We didn't ask people to believe what we believed in order to live with us, but we did ask them to follow our routines of prayer, work and common meals. We put a lot of effort into caring and personal mealtimes, and it was not unusual to have 10 or 20 guests eating with us. At the end of the meal, we read a few verses from the New Testament and discussed the words of Jesus. We welcomed anyone to make a contribution. Afterward, we sat around the table, drank chai and talked. People were fascinated with our life together. Many of them became followers of Jesus simply by participating in our lifestyle of community and care.

I realized one day that what we were doing in Afghanistan was church. We didn't call it that. There wasn't a sign outside that read "First Church of the Long-Haired Hippies," but we were doing what they did in the book of Acts. I had rebelled against the idea of church but found myself leading a community that was, in fact, a house church based in my own home.

My time in Afghanistan proved to me that, especially for those who refuse to enter a traditional church, house churches are an effective way to communicate the message of Jesus through hospitality in our homes.

House Churches Reproduce Leaders

Each house church is volunteer led by a spiritual father or mother who may function with a small team of other servant leaders.

He or she does not simply lead a meeting, but rather provides an everyday environment in which people can grow spiritually. These leaders are intent on training and reproducing more leadership within the house church (see Acts 14:23). They gently nurture individuals until they are ready to take a step of faith to become leaders themselves. We believe good leadership is coaching others to lead—from the outset.

At one time, my wife and I (Floyd) were part of a home church that went through one crisis after another. At one point, the group almost dissolved because of some hurt feelings, offended relationships and people leaving the group. Then, two couples started giving some leadership to our home church. Their goal wasn't to be *the* leaders. They just met a need. They didn't want the group to fall apart. These two couples are not superstars, nor do they want to be. Both couples have experienced the superstar-type syndrome and are glad to be free of it.

Bob and Susan were part of a transcendental cult for many years. Bob was a monk who spent hours every day meditating—until he and Susan found Jesus. Bryan, on the other hand, gave years of his life to serving as a leader in a Charismatic church and finally burned out. He was deeply wounded by the rules, hype and control. Today he and his wife, Sharon, just want to be part of a genuine community of friends who love each other. Bryan wrestled with the sense of calling he once had on his life. He missed preaching the Word, but he was committed to living out his calling in the marketplace as part of a community of friends. Neither couple was infatuated with being a "house church." They just loved Jesus and people and took joy in sharing Jesus with neighbors and workmates.

In house church, the leaders that are trained don't have to be seminary graduates. They never have to worry about losing their jobs . . . because they will never have one. In other words, the key to passing the torch to the next generation of leaders in micro-churches is not structuring it around salaried pastoral positions. This is a new style of leadership that requires serving behind the scenes and being secure enough to be a coach to new leaders without position or title. The goal of leadership in a house-church planting movement is not to be up-front leaders or elders but to be spiritual fathers or mothers to a movement of elders and church planters.

House-Church Networks

House church doesn't always mean small church. Rather, house church includes celebration in large gatherings whenever possible. There is a place for large meetings, because they encourage people to remember that they are part of something bigger than themselves. Large celebrations inspire faith and point the way forward for the whole congregation or network of churches.

Several new micro-church leaders we know (many in their 20s and 30s) say that their communities meet with other community and house churches in their area once every month or so for corporate worship and teaching, because they recognize the need to be connected. This desire to network comes from a similar desire—the desire to receive oversight from spiritual fathers and mothers in order to stay accountable. When each house church, although a little church in itself, is committed to networking (more in chapter 15) with other micro-churches in their city or region, it keeps them from pride, exclusiveness and heresy (more in chapter 14).

Zdero's Canadian network of house churches has grown throughout the years to include regional networks that are organized to help home churches with logistical issues such as how to organize a weekly gathering and how to pool resources for charity work (like helping developing countries or the disadvantaged closer to home). Though offering assistance, the

networks make a point of not acting as spiritual guides, handing down spiritual interpretations or edicts, as might be expected from a church's central organization. "Each home church
remains a self-governing unit," Zdero says.[4]

LaVerne and I (Larry) are involved in a different micro-
church network in Lancaster County. Several years ago, a
group of 20-year-olds began to meet weekly to pray about
starting a new type of church to reach their generation. We
opened our home for this new group to start their first church,
and served as coaches to a younger group of leaders. Today,
this first house church has multiplied and grown into six
house churches and is called the Lancaster Micro-Church
Network (LMCN). The network inspires others in our community to take a step of faith and start their own micro-churches
and micro-church networks. These house churches meet weekly to share life together, and they gather for a larger celebration
every month. The LMCN is important because most of those
in our micro-church are first-generation believers who would
never fit into a conventional church.

Some house churches include several smaller groups within
the house church. These small groups meet regularly outside of
the regular house-church meeting times for prayer, encouragement and accountability. One cell of people may regularly meet
for breakfast before work and another cell may meet together
to disciple a few new Christians. Smaller groups like this help to
foster deeper relationships and greater accountability as they
become involved in a lifestyle of everyday community.

Relationships Minus Bureaucracy

A healthy house church models a way of life, not a formal bureauc-
racy. It takes place outside of the mentality of religious meetings.
Church is the people living their lives in an extended spiritual

family as they focus on discipling and mentoring one another and reaching out to those who don't follow Jesus. House churches, like families, do require some organization, but it is generally relational in nature rather than stiff and governmental.

Years of traditions since the Early Church have made the Church very complicated. Perhaps God is calling us back to the simplicity of the New Testament church. Psychologist Larry Crabb, in his book *Connecting*, astutely remarks:

> Maybe the center of Christian community is connecting with a few, where ordinary Christians, whose lives regularly intersect, will accomplish most of the good that we now depend on professionals to provide. That will happen as people connect with each other in ways that only the gospel makes possible.[5]

Sounds pretty simple, doesn't it? We need those relational connections in church life. They should be at its very core. In healthy, thriving micro-churches, people's lives can and should easily and regularly intersect.

Vision from God for church in its simplest form is a powerful thing. Church is people, ordinary people, living their lives for Jesus. No hype, no being mad at anyone, no special revelation or new doctrine or wonder-leader—it's just friends obeying Jesus together. Do you want to be part of a church community that is relationally and intentionally reaching out to others? That is what church is all about.

Don't Isolate! Find the Connection

Some words of warning: House churches (and churches of any kind, for that matter) should never be exclusive entities cut off from the rest of the Body of Christ. It is true that some people have started house churches because they were disillusioned, hurt or bitter at the churches they were a part of. These people meet in their homes, certain that they are right and that the rest of the Church is wrong.

There are entire books that advocate this type of unwholesome behavior. "We must beware of authors who live in anger toward the established church," says Ralph Moore, who is responsible for planting dozens of Hope Chapel churches throughout Hawaii and the West Coast of the U.S. "The anger of man still can't work the righteousness of God."[6] We totally agree.

The litmus test used to discern if a house church is healthy is simple: The believers in a healthy house church focus on loving Jesus, loving each other, reaching those who don't know Jesus and respecting the rest of the Body of Christ.

We need each other. God offers a breadth of richness through different Christian faith expressions. Each kind of church contributes its strengths to the others and God uses different types of churches to accomplish His purposes. Each part of the Church, regardless of denominational labels or structure, is a part of the Body of Christ. God works through all of His people, giving us a sense of the broader community of Christ's Body.

Notes
1. This quote and the following extra notes concerning the local church are taken from an e-mail excerpt from Joel Comiskey that was sent to Larry Kreider:

> **Elders and leadership** (see Acts 14:21-23; 1 Tim. 3)—Hebrews 13:17 says to obey your leaders and submit to their authority. Even though Paul called the Church a church before elders were appointed, his goal was always to appoint elders and God-ordained leadership.

Under the Lordship of Christ—Ephesians 5, Romans 14 and many other places in the Bible say that any biblical church must be under His Lordship.

Mutual accountability to one another—1 Corinthians 12-14, Romans 12, and other places in the Bible talk about each member functioning as an organic part of Christ's Body through the gifts of the Spirit. So, we are accountable to each other. And in order to be accountable to each other, we have to know each other at a local level. Accountability includes church discipline to keep the Body pure (see 1 Cor. 5; Gal. 6:1-2), which also implies that we must know each other on a local level.

Participation in the sacraments (see Matt. 28:18-20; 1 Cor. 11; the Gospels)—Jesus talked about coming together as His Body to celebrate His death and resurrection. He also told His Church to make disciples through baptism. These two functions should take place in the local church and define a key reason for its existence.

2. David Garrison, *Church Planting Movements* (Bangalore, India: WIGTake Resources, 2004), p. 271.
3. Rad Zdero, Ph.D., *The Global House Church Movement* (Pasadena, CA: William Carey Library Press, 2004), p. 2.
4. Ibid.
5. Larry Crabb, *Connecting* (Nashville, TN: W Publishing Group, 1997), p. xii.
6. Ralph Moore, *House2House Magazine,* March 2001, p. 20.

CHAPTER 7

EVERY GENERATION NEEDS THEIR OWN FORM OF CHURCH

A young man in his mid-twenties poured out his frustrations to me after I (Larry) spoke at his church, a thriving mega-church in the U.S. "I have been a staff member of this church for the past few years," he said. "I've not told anyone yet, but I'm planning to quit and move on to something else. I can't take it anymore. This is a great church, and I love the leaders. But they are too busy. If just one of them gave me only one hour a month to have breakfast with me and hear my heart, I would stay. What I really want is a spiritual father. I just don't feel I fit in here. So, I'm going to leave. Even though good things are happening here, it is just not me. I must take a step of faith and find my way. There has to be more."

Like many of today's youth, this young person was searching for authenticity, community and simplicity in church, but he wasn't finding it. Instead, he felt like he was playing a game because of the highly polished church services, the hierarchy of church leadership and the lack of felt community. Young people are pursuing alternative ideas of how to do church—not because they are looking for an easier faith, but because they are searching for a more interactive, informal community that challenges them.

Lindsey, 26, is a graphic designer who had given up on church after high school. "I'd go to churches that were way too judgmental or ambiguous," she said. Now that she is part of one of the emerging small churches, she is able to see church as a different kind of community: "There is no question what we're doing. We're talking about Jesus. We're taking communion. We're just doing it together, as a journey."[1]

While the Baby Boomers found their strength in numbers (whether at Woodstock or in mega-churches), today's generation is much more interested in relational communities where everyone knows each other. New kinds of churches fit the heart, call and passions of young adults. Micro-churches especially appeal to young adults because they offer the kind of relational church experience to which they can relate.

Changing the Way We Do Church

In his book *Boiling Point*, George Barna, a specialist in research on the Christian Church and its effectiveness in our culture, takes an in-depth look at the changing beliefs and attitudes of society today and how Christians must anticipate the world's spiritual needs. One of the innovations he suggests for doing church is to offer the house church as a structure for restoring community and authenticity:

> Popular in other countries, especially Southeast Asia, thousands of independent faith groups will meet for a complete church experience and expression within living rooms and garages . . . this option will appeal to individuals who are especially interested in restoring authenticity, community and simplicity to the church.[2]

Barna's extensive studies of the prevailing culture have caused him to see that the Church today is failing to fulfill the needs of today's generation. The Church is failing today's youth because of its gaping deficiencies. In his more recent book, *Revolution*, Barna says that the two younger generations of

Americans—the Baby Busters (those born from 1965 through
1983) and the Mosaics (born from 1984 through 2002)—are
"altering the ways in which people relate to each other . . .
radically affecting how people perceive and practice their faith
. . . [and] have little patience for anything based on tradition,
customs, ease, or social acceptability. If they do not immediately sense the relevance of something, they dismiss it out of hand
and move on to the next alternative."[3]

This kind of worldview affects the ways we understand and
practice Christianity and may also cause the Church to undergo a
face change. "Just wait for it," says Karsten Wolf, a youth pastor
from Germany who believes that the youth culture churches of
today will define the Church of the future. Consider the following:

- Generation X (Baby Busters) worldwide is the largest
  single generation in the history of mankind, number-
  ing almost two billion.

- The media is beaming the same message to the same
  generation worldwide. Young people (ages 18 to 35) are
  more uniform in their thinking today than ever before.

- As this generation ages and—within the next decade—
  decides the prevailing culture, they will bring their
  changes with them. Whatever this generation has done
  to the Church will be lasting and normative.

"The young people of today . . . will be the society of the
nations," says Wolf. "That's why . . . youth culture churches may
well revolutionize what church becomes in the future. We could
be looking at an absolutely new form of church."[4]

Wolf and others agree that youth culture churches are high
on relationships and low on structure. Throughout our travels

around the world, we have come to similar conclusions, noticing that this generation has four basic values—each of which is ideally realized and experienced in micro-church communities.

The Four Basic Values of Churches

Brothers Mike and Will Stoltzfus were only 21 and 19 when they joined a few friends to start a weekly meeting for young people in Lancaster County, Pennsylvania. Their group grew rapidly to 1,000 strong. Several people out of this group eventually planted other micro-churches in various places in the county. Will and Mike had started the Lancaster Micro-Church Network (LMCN). Will has since moved to California and Mike continues to lead the LMCN team. The values that are important to Mike and Will and what they believe their generation is looking for in the Church can be summarized as *relationship, authenticity, the freedom to be creative* and *intergenerational connection*:

Relationship
Young adults appreciate being with others to whom they can connect. Hanging out with friends is of high value to them. When a few of Mike's and Will's friends led several people to Jesus, they didn't do it in church or at a church function. They simply began to spend time with pre-Christians, and through their times together were able to share Jesus. The new believers are now growing and being discipled through natural relationships.

Authenticity
Young adults are tired of the plastic, smiling Christianity where things look good on the surface but underneath aren't real. They are looking for people who are real and who live out their Christianity authentically every day. Many times, non-Christians are more open and honest with each other than Christians.

A friend of Mike's and Will's who recently made a decision to follow Christ still spends time with many non-Christians. He says that one of the things that he enjoys about his unchurched friends is how they spend time together and are open about their lives.

The Freedom to Be Creative

Young adults also have a strong desire to see creativity within the Church. God has given us creative minds and hearts. Sadly enough, even when we desire to see creativity, our current structures make it a hard thing to release. The larger our groups get, the harder it is to be creative and flexible. We must have avenues that don't compromise biblical truth and where people can express who they are.

Intergenerational Connection

Due to the staggering number of young people both inside and outside of the Church who do not have true fathers and mothers in their lives, there is a strong desire to connect with those who are older. Some people have dubbed today's younger people as "the fatherless and motherless generations." The enemy has ravaged us with this breakdown of family life, and it has left many feeling hopeless, lost and insecure. God is using that void, however, to turn the hearts of spiritual fathers and mothers to spiritually hungry young people, and He is turning the hearts of those young people to the fathers and mothers. Many will come into the Kingdom because of their connections with spiritual fathers and mothers who naturally exhibit these four values.

Let's Empower Our Young People!

Many of the younger generation in our churches desire to experience something new. They are no longer satisfied with the church structure of their present and prior experience. We have the opportunity to encourage them to build their own structures and to reproduce church as they imagine it. A few years ago, Rick Joyner from Charlotte, North Carolina, told a group of pastors in Pennsylvania, "Pastors sometimes don't like having young stallions in their churches. They seem to cause too many problems. But only young stallions can reproduce. Resist the temptation to 'fix' them so that they cannot reproduce!"

Young adults aged 18 to 35 have often told me (Larry) that they like their churches and pastors, but that their present churches are not something they want to give their lives for. They lead cell groups, youth groups and serve in the church, but they don't want to do those things for their whole lives. God is calling them to something new—to new kinds of church. They're not even sure what it will look like, but they want the opportunity to try. They are not rebellious. They want the blessing of the leaders of their churches. They respect and honor them, but they want to build their own houses. There are things the Lord has placed inside of them that they desire to see become realities. It is good to have a room within their father's house, but they have a God-given desire to build a new home.

I (Larry) understand completely. I remember how I felt when I was in my 20s and the Lord called me to start a new church—a new wineskin. During the early 1980s, when I was a new pastor, new churches were springing up everywhere in our area. The majority of the leaders were in their early 20s. Barry Wissler, who pastors Ephrata Community Church in Ephrata, Pennsylvania, and who oversees Harvest-Net, a new apostolic network of churches, was only 20 when he planted a new church. I was in my late 20s when I planted a church. A word to us oldsters: Let's not forget where we came from!

The reality is this: New wineskins eventually get old. We believe that God often places a burden in the younger generations to pioneer new churches because they have a different vision for a different era and a different generation. The younger generations come into God's kingdom looking for reality, not religious structures. They want relationships, not outdated church programs. Let's help them start the new church structures that fit the needs of their generation.

Not Only for the Younger Generation!

We emphasize that, although the model of a church as a simple community appeals especially to the young, there are thousands of other "young at heart" people with the same vision burning in *their* hearts. Many believers, especially in North America, have spent the past 20 to 30 years with a sense of unrest in their spirits. They love the Lord, but are discouraged. A couple of decades ago, they experienced a new wave of the Spirit sweeping across North America. Out of this renewal, they envisioned a radical New Testament church experience, but cumbersome church structure and traditional church meetings and procedures frustrated the dream. Now they find themselves in a holding pattern. They dream of experiencing life-changing discipleship that transforms society around them, but they are not experiencing anything close to it right now.

Deep in their spirits, they believe that the Lord is about to make some radical changes in His Church. They have been looking for something new, yet they remain unsure of what they are looking for. They are passionately in love with Jesus but are unable to find their niche in the Body of Christ.

Hundreds of thousands—perhaps even millions—of these seasoned believers are being positioned by the Lord to open their homes and start new micro-churches in their communities. That which they have dreamed about for many years will be accomplished through their obedience. If you fit into this category, be encouraged. The best is yet to come.

Notes

1. John Leland, "Hip New Churches Pray to a Different Drummer," *The New York Times,* February 18, 2004.
2. George Barna and Mark Hatch, *Boiling Point* (Ventura, CA: Regal, 2001), p. 250.
3. George Barna, *Revolution* (Wheaton, IL: Tyndale House Publishers, 2005), pp. 42, 44.
4. Karsten Wolf, "Will Youth Culture Churches Define the Church of the Future?" DAWN European Network, 2002. http://www.dawneurope.net/Karsten.htm (accessed December 2006).

CHAPTER 8

HOW TO "BE THE CHURCH"

Y ou don't have to be a rocket scientist to understand how house churches function. In fact, if you remember these five steps: *pray, meet, make, gather* and *multiply*, you are well on your way to understanding how to be the Church. These steps work in any generation and any social strata. We don't need to change the basic principles of church because the culture is different—the forms and structures may change as needed, but the grounding principles are the same.

Let us tell you the story of a young couple and their friends who started a church in their homes by following these five truths. This couple intentionally reached out to their neighbors. They decided to hang out mostly with non-Christians. They immediately got involved in the lives and activities of people around them, including people at work and school. As they did so, they spent a lot of time in prayer, asking God to lead them to people who were spiritually open. They invited their new friends into their homes for meals and hanging out. In six months, they had a seekers Bible study going, plus a circle of friends and acquaintances who were asking deeper questions. For those who didn't show interest in more than the Bible study, they continued with the regular social events in their home. Whenever someone did show interest in going deeper, they met with that person individually, and if he or she showed even more interest, that person was invited to a discussion group.

Did you observe the natural progression of what they did? They *prayed*, they *met* people, they *made disciples* by investing in the lives of those who were seeking answers to spiritual questions, and as they *gathered* people in their homes, they selected potential leaders and prepared to *multiply* by starting a new discussion group.

A U.S. businessman named William was making $350,000 a year but was bored. To alleviate his boredom, Bill decided to go and serve the poor in the Indian sub-continent. During a time of prayer, Bill felt the Lord saying that he should invest his time in discipling a young man who was a paraplegic. After a couple of years spent in training him, Bill encouraged this man to start a church for his friends, many of whom were also in wheelchairs. These were people who nobody wanted—the outcasts (one of the lowest castes in Hindu society), the lepers, the homeless and the disabled.

Bill, meanwhile, started businesses to employ the "unemployable," giving life skills and training to people who otherwise had nothing going for them. I (Floyd) attended their church, called Beautiful Gate, recently and witnessed 200 people crammed into a small room for a celebration involving seven of their house churches around Kathmandu. All the elders were sitting in front, and all were wheelchair-bound. During the worship time, I saw people with missing fingers raising their hands. Others had missing noses and ears—all due to leprosy. Despite their affliction, the joy of the Lord was there and the people were worshiping Him with all their hearts. It was an absolutely moving and gorgeous scene to witness.

Bill provides coaching and spiritual oversight from behind the scenes. He told me, "We pray everyday, go to the poor, I disciple people and pour my life into them, we encourage them to gather in small home groups, and, as soon as we can, we multiply." There, I heard it again—the five things they do to make it a success. They *prayed* for those they *met* who did not yet know Jesus, *discipled* them, *gathered* them into their homes, and *multiplied*.

Why make it so hard? Church only takes five simple steps—not always easy steps, but simple and straightforward.

Pray

Why pray? Because church, any form of church, is God's way of reclaiming lives for His kingdom. We are building people up to be lovers of Jesus, and the enemy hates that. He will oppose us. If we don't pray, we will lose touch with our source of power for the battle.

Prayer is also about intimacy. It's about being more in love with Jesus by spending time with Him. When we don't pray, our faith level goes down. When we pray, we hear from God.

It's in those intimate times with Jesus that we get fresh revelation, not only for ourselves, but also for those we are reaching out to—those we are gathering and nurturing. The Lord puts love in our hearts for a few people we can pour our lives into and mentor.

When Sally and I (Floyd) first moved to the red-light district of Amsterdam in the 1980s, there were only five evangelical churches in the city. A survey was done after we left Amsterdam in the 1990s and we were amazed to discover that the number of churches (including house churches) there had risen to 400. I believe we helped shape history in that city.

During one prayer meeting, we asked the Lord how we should pray for the city of Amsterdam. We were impressed to pray for "a drug famine" in this, the notorious drug capital of the world. Two weeks later the headlines in the news were: "Drug Famine Hits Amsterdam." You should have heard the jubilation in our community: "We did that!" Prayer was the key.

Our agenda as the Church of Jesus Christ is to reclaim the broken people and broken marriages that the enemy has taken captive, and to bring them into a community—a safe place where they can grow and find Jesus. We are called to join God on His redemptive mission. Prayer is where we must gain compassion and the energy necessary to live out this mission.

Before the birth of the Lancaster Micro-Church Network lead by me (Larry), the leadership team prayed for two years before starting the first micro-church. We knew we needed a word from God—a strategy from heaven, not just a good idea. The young leaders wanted to be properly commissioned out of their community churches, knowing that the Lord's timing was paramount. And laying a foundation of prayer paid off. When the first micro-church started, the Lord had prepared a whole group of young adults who were open to the good news about Jesus and who came to Christ within the first six months of the new church being planted. Eventually, the LMCN was commissioned by the leadership of their churches, and the Christian leaders of our community recognized it as a valid house-church network. It pays to pray and wait for the timing of God.

Meet People

Do not hang out with Christians! Strange as it may sound, this is the direction we often give people when they start a new house church. Or at least, do not spend *all* of your time with Christians. Since micro-churches do not have a lot of meetings to go to, programs to maintain or buildings to pay for, those involved in the micro-church have more time to engage their hearts and lives with a few people in spiritual community *and* with a lot of people who don't know Jesus.

We must be intentional in order to develop friendships with non-Christians. We can get involved in adult sports leagues or attend our children's sporting events to meet members of the community. We can join an art class or archery club. We can initiate a summer block party in our neighborhood or get involved in a community project or serve at a soup kitchen. These are all great ways we can develop friendships with people who don't follow Jesus. And as we hang out with pre-Christians, we can pray for them. We know the God who made them, so we can ask Him to reveal His love for them to us as we pray.

Even aside from prayer, we carry God into each relationship we develop. We are not at work on our jobs or attending school just to be there—we are there with the living word of God breathing in our spirits with hope and faith and compassion for the people with whom we interact. And in those relationships and others, prayer allows us to see people differently.

One time, I (Floyd) was standing in a line at a restaurant buffet, and I could sense the pain in the girl serving me. It was palpable and heartbreaking. I felt I had to say something. So I said, "We are soon going to be seated, and when we thank God for our food, is there something we could pray about for you? If there is one thing you want from God right now in your life, what would it be?"

She looked at me, hung her head for a moment, then looked up and said, "I am desperate for peace in my life." Heaven came right there in that moment! It was a divine connection in a very ordinary time and place. I wasn't there to sell God to her or persuade her of His goodness. God simply showed me her pain and I obeyed His prompting to reach out to her.

Likewise, Jesus didn't come to sell us something. He came to offer Himself. Evangelism is about *giving*—it's about giving to people. I have since talked to that girl when I've returned to the buffet, and we've had wonderful conversations. I haven't seen her come to Jesus, but I did say and do what God asked of me at the time.

God gives us so many opportunities in everyday life to speak for Him and to explain His love. My wife, Sally, is the chocolate-chip-cookie-baker queen of all time and she gives the cookies she bakes to all the shopkeepers in our neighborhood—from the dry-cleaner to the gasoline station owner. She exercises her gift of encouragement through praying for people and giving gifts to them.

When we returned to Amsterdam to visit after many years of absence from the city, I was surprised to see how many friends Sally had made in the city. I thought I had been the main evangelist back then, but Sally, in her quiet way, had made many more contacts—not through overt evangelism but through friendship. A case in point: When we walked into a chocolate shop in Amsterdam that we hadn't visited in 11 years, the shopkeeper looked at Sally and screamed with joy as she threw her arms around her. She called for her boss to come to the shop. Sally later told me she had prayed with him when his marriage had fallen apart and when he was a broken man. They loved my wife because through her they saw a different picture of God than they had known before. In this way, Sally had simply used her passions and gifts to share Jesus with others.

We suggest that you make a list of three to four people and begin to pray for them. God wants to use you to birth house churches out of prayer and intentional time spent with people who don't know Jesus.

All it takes is one person to come to Christ from an unchurched background, and he or she will bring a whole host of other people who don't know Jesus. Our house church in Pennsylvania is the product of a few people who came to Christ and then brought their friends along. Even Jesus evangelized in this way—He built friendships and His friends brought their friends to meet Him. Remember the woman at the well? One woman whom Jesus befriended introduced Christ to the entire town!

Make Disciples

Jesus prayed this prayer at the end of His life on Earth: "The words you have given to me I have given to the men you have given me" (John 17:8). He invested Himself in others. He coached and encouraged them.

Who are the men and women God has given you? He has people just for you. House church is about intentionally investing in other peoples' lives. If we are meeting with those people, pouring into them, praying together, and growing together, we don't have to worry about our micro-churches turning into little, selfish holy huddles. Instead, we will be growing, dynamic, Jesus-following, Jesus-obeying, Spirit-led communities.

If we have problems with people sitting around nitpicking and complaining in our churches, we must get those people going for God. We've learned by experience that if you want people to grow, you have to motivate them to make disciples, to pray for people and to be outward-focused. Common sense tells you that it doesn't work to put kids in a room and say, "Have fun for the next five hours." No, we must get them outwardly focused: "Let's play a game." We give them a goal, and they play better together because they have been given a common *mission*.

Did you realize that disciple making does not have to start *after* people become Christians? If you really think about it, there's no biblical difference between *discipleship* and *evangelism*. This point can turn your paradigm upside down! Listen to this story: Bill was working in Amman, Jordan, with a church-planting team. He also had a circle of Muslim friends. The church-planting team started meeting together in Bill's house to pray for their community. One day, one of Bill's Muslim friends discovered that people were meeting regularly at Bill's house and he wondered why he was not invited. In his mind, they were "secret" meetings, and in Muslim culture, the home is always open and welcome to friends. Friends don't have secret meetings.

So Bill's friend came to him and asked, "Why haven't you told me about this meeting in your home? May I attend?" Now imagine, the church-planting team was meeting to strategize and pray about how they could reach the Muslim people in the community . . . and a Muslim man wanted to attend. Bill assured his friend that he could attend, meanwhile telling the church-planting team not to speak in "Christianese" so that his friend would feel more at home. At the first meeting Bill's friend attended, the group met together over a meal, and then had a short Bible study from the Sermon on the Mount. They sang together and talked about the words of Jesus. Afterward, the Muslim friend said, "I really enjoyed that. May I come again?"

"Sure," Bill said, "And this time, you lead the discussion."

"But what will I say?" the Muslim friend wondered.

Bill assured him, "I'll meet with you before the meeting and we'll discuss it. And I'll give you some books to read beforehand."

At the next meeting, a Muslim led a Christian church-planting team in a Bible study! The next week, Bill's Muslim friend said to him, "How did I do? I didn't quite understand what Jesus meant when He said those words." It was an open door, and Bill and his Muslim friend continued many months of studying the words of Jesus together. Today, that Muslim friend is a leader in a small community of Jesus followers.

Notice that Bill started mentoring his friend *before* he chose to follow Jesus. Discipleship can start before people become Christians, because discipleship is really just a spiritual journey of sharing Jesus, of loving people, of planting a seed of faith and of inviting people into a love relationship with Jesus.

If our micro-churches are not highly religious, and if we speak in common language instead of Christianese, people who are not yet Christians will be free to come and join us. They will feel at home with other *normal* people. If we gather primarily around food and fellowship, people from all walks of faith and life just naturally fit in.

Gather

Food is an important part of a micro-church. People who would never think to step inside a traditional church will accept an invitation for a meal in your home, a picnic at a park or coffee at a café. New Zealander, Tony Collis says:

> Families eat together, and so does the family of God. For the early church, the dinnertime became the love feast during which time they celebrated communion. While they ate together, they shared victories, challenges and insights. As they consumed they communed. Still today we build relationships over cappuccino at cafés or pizzas in the park. Strangers become friends after only a few minutes eating together, because what can go wrong over some food? In our first ever micro-church meeting, the hostess had a visitor who stayed on for a short time to get a handle on who we were and what we were doing. She was invited to stay and enjoy the meal, of which she did. By the end of the evening she became a new member of the group. Food had made a friend.[1]

We (Larry) always have food at our micro-church meetings. Our church meets on Wednesday nights beginning at 6:30 P.M. with food. Everyone is encouraged to bring something, and we eat whatever we have. We often say, "Church has begun," when we begin to eat. Eating together is a very important part of church. That is why the New Testament church met from house to house and shared meals together. They were experiencing true family and authentic community—they shared meals and life together, rather than just sitting in a pew, seeing the back of somebody's head once a week.

We don't have to *package* the house-church meetings. There's no need to have a guitar, five songs and a sermon. If all we are doing is reducing a traditional Sunday service into a smaller meeting on a weekday, then what we are doing is rather pointless.

I (Floyd) have a friend who, some years ago, tried to start a house church and failed. Recently he asked me, "What do you think about house churches, Floyd?" I started to talk about facilitating leadership and community and sharing and not being religious. As I spoke, he became more and more quiet. Finally, he groaned—loudly!

"What's wrong," I asked.

"Oh," he groaned again. "Floyd, I did it all wrong. I just wanted to teach so much. We started our group and I just taught from the Word. One night, after a few months, one of my closest friends interrupted me right in the middle of my teaching and said, 'I just can't take this anymore. If I wanted to sit and listen to someone talk, I'd have kept attending Sunday morning church services.'"

My friend was deeply hurt by this experience. His struggle was with the format of the gathering, not an issue of respect for authority—he didn't understand how leaders were supposed to lead a house church. He also didn't understand that the goal of New Testament leadership is to facilitate, release and encourage. The goal of a good teacher is not to do all the teaching but to get others to do the teaching, to get a learning and discovering discussion going and to get the Word into people's lives.

When we gather around food and hang out together, we *do* lead, but we lead as *facilitators*. We advise house-church *facilitators* not to call themselves *pastors*. We don't want the paradigm of top-down, hierarchical, Old Testament-style leadership. Look at Jesus: He was very much a leader in that He spoke with authority. He could say, "Here are the boundaries; here's where we are going," but He exercised His authority from *beside*, not from *above*. He didn't have to have a title of "pastor" or "priest" to lead. He was not interested in getting a meeting established— He wanted a movement to be born! He was going for the long haul, the big picture. He modeled a style of leadership that facilitated many leaders and participants.

Multiply

Everything in life will multiply: plants, rabbits, bacteria . . . and life-giving micro-churches. We must expect at the outset that our micro-church will multiply. It is only through multiplication that we will experience the fulfillment of the Great Commission.

I (Larry) have a friend who was leading a group of believers in his home but found that he and his wife were doing everything. He came to our training school for church planters, and I encouraged him to give responsibilities away to others. So he made a list of everything he and his wife were doing—including opening their home, leading the Bible study discussion and all the other tasks they did each week to keep their house group alive. When he offered the other members of the group the opportunity to serve, he was shocked—they took everything! But that's not the end of the story: Over the course of about six months, that single group of believers multiplied into three groups—a prime example that God's people learn by doing!

The beauty of house church is that we can dream big *and build small*. We draw people into small gatherings, spot one or two people to train and then encourage those people to be leaders. Some of these leaders may fall away. But be encouraged! Keep pouring your life into others. A very wise man once said, "Throw water on the ground and tend the flowers where they grow." To avoid discouragement, we must concentrate our efforts where growth is occurring.

Pour your heart into others. We know two church-planting couples that work together in a house church. One couple does most of their leading from behind the scenes. The other couple rarely says anything at the meetings. Both couples have trained others to lead communion, lead in song and organize food so that they can be available to coach and encourage from the sidelines. As we teach others to serve, the Holy Spirit causes the churches to multiply. Sometimes our house churches never multiply because we get in the way. Let's get out of the way!

Successful house churches follow the example of Jesus and imitate the natural progression of what He did. He *prayed*, He *met* people, He *made* disciples as He *gathered* them close to Himself, and then He selected leaders to *multiply* the impact of His kingdom.

Note

1. Tony Collis, *A New Wineskin* (Lower Hutt, New Zealand: Jubilee Resources, 2002), p. 9.

CHAPTER 9

HOW TO START A HOUSE CHURCH

House churches are not organizations that require people with administrative skills or immense giftedness to coordinate and direct a group—they simply call for ordinary people who are in love with Jesus. Neil Cole, in *Cultivating a Life for God*, believes that simplicity is the key to fulfilling the Great Commission. He says, "The more complex the process, the greater the giftedness needed to keep it going."[1] The really good news is that, to start a house church, you can lay down the burdens of planning how to cope with buildings, programs and outreach strategies. You don't have to be an impressive leader (though you probably will have some leadership gifts). To start a house church, you simply need to open your home to friends and neighbors and take things one step at a time.

Pray First!

In the last chapter, we learned that the first step to starting a house church is to pray. House-church ministry *must* be birthed in prayer. Though it is a simple step, without prayer and God's leading, we invite trouble. Starting a house church cannot be just a good idea; it must be a *God* idea. If you feel that you are called to start a house church, gather a few like-minded people together and begin to pray so that you can receive a strategy from God. Many house churches have false starts that are directly linked to a lack of prayer.

Taking time to pray gives God the opportunity to work in our hearts and purify our motives. When house churches start up because of a reaction to something we don't like about the established church, the house church's identity is built from rebellion and discord. Healthy house churches, on the contrary, must begin with God's leading and a desire to reach those who don't know Jesus. What a person sows, the Bible teaches us, he also reaps. Therefore, if you begin a house church because of an offense toward an existing church or leader, you will sow the seeds of fault finding and pride in the church you are creating.

Along with prayer, it is also important to look to the local Christian community's leaders for spiritual guidance and advice as you launch a new church. From day one of the LMCN house-church network, we have cultivated relationships with established believers in our local community and beyond to answer questions and explain to them the concept of micro-church. A wise Bible teacher once said, "Lone rangers get shot out of the saddle." We agree. Healthy house-church movements are not exclusive groups who refuse to be accountable. Vibrant micro-church networks are spiritually connected to leadership in the Body of Christ.

Know Whom You Are Called to Reach

Every micro-church should know whom they are called to reach. Here's a great suggestion from Tony and Felicity Dale who together started a successful network of house churches in Texas:

> Draw together people from your circle of influence. We had a number of business associates who were not Christian, but whom we had come to know pretty well over a period of months or years. We asked a dozen of them to join us in a study of business principles while enjoying pizza in our home, using the book of Proverbs as our textbook. There were no rules to our discussion;

everybody's opinion was valid and there was no such thing as a wrong answer. Gradually we introduced prayer and worship and over the course of a year, every one of them became a Christian. They formed the nucleus of our original house church.[2]

When the first micro-church in the Lancaster Micro-Church Network started in our (Larry and LaVerne's) home a few years ago, we asked God for pre-Christians or new believers to join us—we also asked for laborers to help in the endeavor. However, we ran into some immediate problems. First of all, lots of believers wanted to come and check it out. Some of these Christians were looking for the latest Christian fad. They liked the idea that the micro-church met on a Wednesday, not a Sunday, and that it met in a living room, not a sanctuary.

But we were not starting something new for the sake of starting something new! Since we had a mandate from the Lord to reach new believers, we asked inquiring Christians not to come to our meetings. Having too many older Christians in the group would make the pre-Christians feel uncomfortable.

Jim Petersen, in his book *Church Without Walls,* clearly describes what can happen if a "migratory flock from neighboring churches" invades a new church simply because they are curious:

I have a friend who was a part of a team that set out to start a church . . . The congregation was divided into house churches, each of which was assigned an elder who helped shepherd the members of that house church. Centralized activities were kept at a minimum for the sake of keeping people free to minister to their families and unbelieving friends.

The weekly meetings were dynamic. I will never forget the first one I visited. People of all sorts were there,

from men in business suits to ponytails. Many were
new believers. The Bible teaching was down to earth,
aimed at people's needs. I loved it.
So did most everyone else who visited. The word got
around and soon the migratory flock from neighboring
churches came pouring in. Their needs consumed the
energies of the leaders of this young church. Their
wants gradually set the agenda. The inertia of the traditions of these migrants engulfed this very creative effort
and shaped it accordingly . . . So what's the problem,
we ask? The problem is that the vision that original
team had for taking the church into society through the
efforts of every believer was frustrated.[3]

LaVerne and I knew that the vision the Lord had given to us
to reach a new generation had to be safeguarded in the early
days of our new micro-church network, and the young leaders
of our network wisely set clear perimeters. They asked God to
bring pre-Christians, new believers and laborers, and the Lord
honored their request.

The Size of the House Church Matters

Quite soon, we (Larry and LaVerne) had a second problem in
our home-based micro-church. The pre-Christians attending
invited their friends, and within six months of starting, we had
50 people in our living room on a given night. It was way too
large! Will and Mike, who led the new house church, appointed other leaders to help them multiply into six or eight smaller
cells. These cell groups met for prayer during part of the house
church meeting so that everyone could experience more intimacy in relationships and vulnerability in prayer, and so that
new believers could be properly discipled.

Very soon the church was so large that it needed to multiply into new house churches, but potential leaders in the group were scared because they felt unequipped to lead a new house church—especially if the new church was going to grow as quickly as this one had! The large house church was the only model they had seen at work, and it was intimidating. Finally, however, two couples were sent to start one new house church and Will took a group with him to start a third church, turning the original church over to Mike. Three smaller micro-churches, rather than one large church, were much healthier and more manageable. With the reorganization that occurred, the network had begun.

Although house churches come in various sizes—depending on the number of people a venue can accommodate as well as the comfort level of a particular group—smaller-sized micro-churches allow for more participation, accountability and commitment, as well as closer interaction and relationships. All in all, a smaller-sized house church lets the group capitalize on its greatest asset—each other!

Rad Zdero, author of *The Global House Church Movement*, agrees that too large of a group may be detrimental:

> It is wise to keep the number of people to between 6 and 12. From my experience, groups less than 6 strong tend to dwindle and be lackluster because of the decreased number of relationships and interactions possible. However, groups over 12 tend to lose intimacy and every-member participation. It is perhaps not surprising, then, that rapid church planting movements today reproduce small house churches numbering between 10 and 30 people.[4]

Frequency of Meeting

House churches should meet at least once a week to maintain a sense of connectedness. Again, though, we must emphasize the importance of flexibility. Some micro-churches meet at the same location every week while others move the meeting place by rotating turns in members' houses. Some groups meet more frequently, others less often. Some house churches meet during the week, others on weekends. It is crucial that meeting together is an expression of the members' desire to build community together and not just a religious duty to add more meetings to their already busy lives. If gathering together is done around food and for the purpose of fellowshipping, it is more natural. Choose times that are convenient for everyone involved and then make an effort to connect with the other members (even just by phone or e-mail) outside of official meeting times. Building a spiritual family takes more than an hour or two one night a week!

Meeting Venue

Some of you reading this book want practical tips and ideas about how a house-church meeting should be conducted. We will try to give you a few ideas, but it is nearly impossible to give an accurate picture of any given gathering, since they can and should change from week to week. One thing is certain: House-church meetings should not be a smaller scale duplicate of a typical Sunday morning meeting. A house-church gathering should not look like an "escaped meeting captured by a living-room," as one young man described house churches that do little more than replicate and repeat the traditional church service format: worship, teaching, prayer.

Instead, we have learned that there are often four basic components to a micro-church gathering: eating, meeting, small groups and "the meeting after the meeting."

1. *Eating:* House-church people love to eat! Everyone should bring food.

2. *Meeting:* House churches gather together for a time
   of worship, teaching and discussion about how the
   Scriptures apply to life.

3. *Small Groups:* If the house church is larger than five
   or six people, we have found small groups to be very
   effective. These groups often meet outside of the
   micro-church meeting. When we ask new believers
   about their favorite part of the micro-church meeting, we hear again and again that they enjoy small
   groups. It is in the context of small groups that new
   believers open up about their lives and learn to pray
   with others for the first time. We have also found
   that gender-specific small groups can be very effective. A house church of eight or ten may have one or
   two small groups of men and one or two small
   groups of women. Oftentimes, house church leaders meet monthly with the small-group leaders for
   training and encouragement. In fact, small-group
   leaders usually become house-church leaders.

4. *The Meeting After the Meeting:* In most conventional
   churches, people are ready to go home right after the
   service. Not so in house church. These people really
   love being together. Actual meeting times may last
   one hour or three or more hours—whatever it takes
   to allow for adequate participation from everyone.

Our (Larry's) house church, for example, begins on
Wednesday nights at 6:30 P.M. The first hour is our time to eat
together, and during the next hour or so we interact with one
another in a time of worship or discussion. We often spend 30
to 45 minutes in small groups, and then many people hang out

for a few hours after the meeting before going home. (After all, being with their spiritual family is a lot like being at home!)

There must be a great flexibility in micro-church ministry— it is necessary in order for the wineskin to contain the new wine. We know of some micro-churches that meet together late Sunday morning and end up spending most of the day together!

Although eating (usually a meal) is one of the elements of a house-church gathering, sometimes there may not be food. One week the house church may help someone trim their shrubs and have a time of prayer afterward, and the next week they may come together for a whole smorgasbord of worship, prayer, teaching and fellowship. Every week should be fresh and informal as people meet to discuss the life of Jesus and life *with* Jesus. Our (Floyd and Sally's) house-church members take turns leading the meetings, each planning something creative for our times together.

We like the practical advice that Tony Collis gives on meeting in a home:

> Do not position your chairs in rows like pews, but in a circle so that everyone is included. If the number of people attending is greater than the number of chairs you have, provide cushions and pillows for those who will end up on the floor.
>
> Please do not bring out your best silver and china as this may make some people uncomfortable and hesitant in making their home available.
>
> Think through how you will respond if a visitor asks if it is fine to smoke. I suggest that whether you are happy for the person to smoke inside or not, that you have available an ashtray to give to the person. By the way, these days it is not offensive to invite the person to have their smoke outside. The provision of an ashtray communicates a

servant spirit and non-judgmental attitude.

. You may want to be playing music when people arrive. Not everyone has the same taste so not everyone will like your choice of music. The main thing is to make sure the music isn't so noisy that it cuts across communication between visitors.[5]

A Mission for Your House Church

Each house church quickly develops its own personality. Some house churches have a knack for helping marriages become healthy, while others are geared toward and led by teens. Still others are good at helping members with practical, day-to-day needs.

Every house church or network should uncover its own vision and mission. For example, the leaders of the micro-church network I (Larry) am a part of designed this vision for our house-church network:

The vision for this house-church network is to create new, flexible wineskins that will be a leadership training ground for rapid reproduction of leaders of small, relational, evangelistic churches. These new churches could meet in homes, campuses, places of business, malls, coffee shops, barns, skate parks, and other places where people naturally meet. Spiritual parents will be trained to mentor new believers, new small-group leaders, new church leaders and new apostolic leaders. The leadership of each church has the freedom and authority to give the church the flavor they sense the Lord directing them to have, within biblical guidelines. These new churches can meet on any day or night of the week and network together by the direction of the Holy Spirit.

The vision and mission of a house church doesn't have to be this long—it could be one sentence: "Our vision is to see house churches within walking distance of every person in our city as we share Jesus with others" or "Our vision is to be an extended family that puts Jesus at the center and reaches out to orphans."

The House Church and Money

Since house churches do not require a lot of organization and administration, they are capable of giving a higher percentage of their income for missions for outreach in developing countries and to those closer to home who are disadvantaged. Without high overheads—building and program maintenance or salaries—house churches and networks of house churches can pool their resources and give a larger percentage of their money to those in need.

> When you think about it, a traditional church of 1,000 members is saddled with a mortgage payment, utilities, janitorial fees, building maintenance and pastoral salaries. However, a network of 1,000 house church people with no staff to pay or buildings to upkeep can give much more. According to a survey of U.S. Protestant congregations, 82 percent of church revenues go to buildings, staff and internal programs, leaving only 18 percent for outreach. With house churches the percentages are reversed![6]

Jim and Cathy Mellon founded the Association of Home Churches in Killeen, Texas. Their network of house churches reports that "We use 80 percent of our income for benevolence and missions; we support 10 local ministries and have planted 220 churches in India. Not bad for a small band of about 100 pioneers!"[7]

Tax Exemption Issues

A question that members will occasionally ask is, "Will my donations to and through my house church be tax deductible?" There are several ways house churches can choose to approach the tax-exempt issue.

Functioning as a single church entity, a house church can legally apply as an individual entity for 501-C3 status. An accountant or attorney can do this for under $1,000. Some very small house churches cannot afford this cost, in which case they may choose to run their finances through an existing Christian entity, such as a network of house churches, a community church or a mega-church. Going through another Christian entity costs a small percentage of total income to cover administration costs. Networked house churches may consider setting up a nonprofit foundation so that they do not have to register each house church in the network as its own nonprofit entity.

In the Lancaster Micro-Church Network (LMCN), each micro-church has the privilege and responsibility to distribute all monies that come in through their tithes and offerings. They can donate money to those in need within their house church, to missions organizations and to the poor in their community and beyond. Each micro-church gives a percentage of their income to the network in order to cover expenses. The LMCN is incorporated, meaning that the individual churches do not have to set up their own incorporations, enabling them to manage their finances through the network. This makes it easier to plant churches and provides financial accountability through yearly audits.

Without the large overhead of buildings and programs, house churches can model how believers share their resources with their community and the Body of Christ. As we love and serve one another, the world sees the love of Jesus.

Pray and Plan to Multiply

Our (Larry and LaVerne's) house church in Pennsylvania has multiplied and planted four new house churches within the past five years. Multiplication and planting new house churches seldom happens naturally. It takes focused prayer, vision-casting and planning ahead.

Our friends Steve and Mary Prokopchak from Elizabeth-town, Pennsylvania, led a home group that ballooned to 85 people a few years ago. The small group kept growing and growing because no one in their home group thought they could lead like Steve and Mary. The Prokopchaks soon realized that they needed to spend more time in developing and encouraging future leaders within their group so that they could multiply.

They approached the problem by breaking into five small prayer groups within the house church and appointing one leader for each group. As house-church leaders, Steve and Mary could then easily mentor the prayer-group leaders. Eventually, the leaders felt confident enough to lead on their own and started to meet in separate homes. Four new house churches were started in a relatively short time, all because the leaders planned ahead and encouraged people to take a step of faith.

As the Prokopchaks' example demonstrates, multiplying is not all that difficult. To aide the growth process, group leaders should continually speak the vision of growth and multiplication. House churches should expect their churches to multiply in the same way that healthy families have an expectation that their children will eventually grow up and start their own families.

In order to foster multiplication, a good leader will focus his or her time and energy on training faithful potential leaders. When they begin, most potential leaders do not think they have what it takes to be leaders. Many potential leaders sit in church pews every Sunday or even attend a small group, unaware that they could be leading a church. They remain inactive because the only church models they have ever seen are the community church model and the mega-church model. They need to be encouraged, equipped and sent out!

We hope you are beginning to realize that community churches and mega-churches are not the only models of church available! The house-church network gives us a new model. It puts everyone on a more even playing field. We believe there are thousands of future house-church leaders who have enough faith to lead 8 to 14 believers in a house-church setting—these are people who would never want to lead 100-plus people or attempt to maintain the many programs and ministries of a traditional church. We believe that the house churches of the future will release a multitude of laborers, who, if it were left up to the traditional church, would never enter the harvest fields of our nation.

Hard Work Required

I (Larry) wish I could say that starting a house church has been easy, but at times it has been very difficult. Discipling new believers and changing spiritual diapers is hard work! In fact, we had to close down one of our micro-churches because the leaders felt overwhelmed. Thankfully, the majority of that group's members joined other micro-churches—some even became part of a future multiplication.

Although it is hard work, micro-church ministry is rewarding. It is extremely gratifying when I see new believers—who would never have become involved in a community church or mega-church—growing in God.

One of my mega-church pastor friends tells me that many of his congregants are only in church once or twice each month. Not so in micro-church! These new believers are very committed to the spiritual family. They seldom miss the house-church gatherings, probably because micro-church is much more than a meeting once a week—it is about sharing life. We help one another move, paint each other's homes, watch movies together, go away on weekends together, and find lots of excuses to have parties. We are a family. Remember, the Church is built through relationships.

Notes
1. Neil Cole, *Cultivating a Life for God* (Saint Charles, IL: ChurchSmart Resources, 1999), p. 35.
2. Felicity Dale, ed., *Getting Started* (Austin, TX: House2House, 2003), p. 86.
3. Jim Petersen, *Church Without Walls* (Colorado Springs, CO: NavPress, 1992), pp. 148-149.
4. Rad Zdero, *The Global House Church Movement* (Pasadena, CA: William Carey Library Press, 2004), p. 94.
5. Tony Collis, *Micro Leadership, Unlocking Small Group Dynamics for Serious Church Growth* (Lower Hutt, New Zealand: Jubilee Resources, 2003), pp. 25-26.
6. Steve Atkerson, ed., *Ekklesia: To the Roots of Biblical Church Life* (Atlanta, GA: New Testament Restoration Foundation, 2005), p. 86.
7. Jim and Cathy Mellon, "Ten Years in a House Church," 2006. http://www.new churches.com/public/church_types/docs/house/ten.pdf (accessed December 2006).

CHILDREN IN HOUSE CHURCHES

O ne of the first questions people who are considering house church ask is, "What do we do with the kids?" There are probably as many answers to this question as there are different kinds of house churches. Every situation will vary according to the number and ages of the children in each house church—some house churches will have one or two children and others will have kids that outnumber adults! In any case, the "kid question" need not send a wave of anxiety over a house church. The Lord values children, and children should take an active role in house-church life.

A house church can offer children a spiritual home and family, a place to belong. Within the house church, children have the opportunity to express love and gratitude to God through worship and praise. They can bond and develop close relationships with other adults in the group. Discipleship can naturally occur in this safe and loving environment. Fruit-bearing seeds are sown in children's lives when they attend house churches, not to mention the fun!

"Neither Jesus, nor the apostles, ever worried about what to do with the children," says Dan Trotter, a house-church leader. He goes on to state:

Jesus never, ever said: "Suffer the little children to be packed away in the nursery." The scripture doesn't say much on handling children when believers gather. I imagine not much was ever said, because the early

Christians didn't make such a big deal about the issue. The churches were in the home; families lived in homes; children met with the church in the home. Although the scriptures don't say anything directly concerning the children and the gatherings of believers, there are glimpses. For example, children are explicitly stated to have been present at the feeding of the five thousand (Matthew 14:21). On a missionary journey, "all the disciples and their wives and children" accompanied the apostles, as they left, to pray on the beach (Acts 21:5).[1]

Jonathan Edwards had it right years ago when he said, "Every Christian family ought to be, as it were, a little church." Integrating children in the house-church mix is easy because house churches are family-oriented. Children bond and develop close relationships with the adults in the group and feel like they are a part of the church family.

Brooke, age 11, who has spent two years in a house church after attending a traditional church, says this about kids in house church: "In big church, we kids sing, go to Sunday School and then leave. But in a house church, kids have a bigger role to play. We feel more important and more involved. Also there is space to be more creative."

Options for Integrating Kids

The perspectives of the parents and other adults in the micro-church play a major role in determining how each individual house church integrates children (see Ps. 22:9-10; Luke 18:16). Just as different cultures do house church differently, so too do individual parents and house-church leaders have various preferences for how to effectively minister to house-church kids. There are often differing opinions on how and when to release

children as effective ministers. Here are some of the many options
to consider.

Family Participation and Children's Ministry Time

It is our observation that the majority of house churches in
North America prefer this option. In this approach, children
join their parents for the first part of the house-church meeting
and meet separately for the second part. While kids are present
in the larger group, they are incorporated into the time of worship, testimonies and prayer. Then they receive their own ministry in another room in the home, or perhaps in a neighboring
home if appropriate.

When children and adults are separated and children are
in another room for a portion of the house-church gathering,
most kids feel honored and cared for. This format also works
well for parents—especially single parents—because it gives
them a break from their children to receive prayer and ministry regarding sensitive family issues.

According to Tony and Felicity Dale, including kids in a portion of their house-church gatherings is chaotic but worth it. In
their network, they try to include the children as much as possible—even in new house churches, like the one they describe here:

> In the second meeting at one of our house churches in
> the projects, ten adults were outnumbered by about
> fifteen kids, varying in age from 18 months to 16 years.
> The majority of these kids had never been to anything
> like this before. As soon as we arrived, the kids we knew
> jumped up to greet us, wanting to choose a song to
> sing and trying to teach their favorite ones to their
> friends. It was chaos! When the meal was over, some-
> one started strumming their guitar, and the kids sang
> their hearts out . . .

When the moment came for us to spend time in discussion around the Bible, a couple of older teens, who had come with us because they love church in the projects, went out to play with some of the kids, while the adults had some time on their own. Initially, there was a bit of traffic in and out, and we had to ask the kids if they would stay outside until we had finished. But eventually they settled down.[2]

Who ministers to the children when they meet separately for the second half of the meeting? Whatever works! Here are some ideas: a rotation of all adult house-church members; responsible, trustworthy older kids; a rotation of couples with children; or teams composed of one parent and another adult (so that the other parent can participate in the discussion). Some house churches share children's services and resources with other house churches. For example, a person with a call to children's ministry might teach the kids in a house church that meets at a different time than his or her own group. In some cases, a house church will bless a non-member who comes in to minister to their children with a generous monetary gift.

Whatever option your house church chooses together, the point is to keep unity and continuity in the group. And, of course, it is tantamount to make sure certain standards are followed to ensure the safety of the children at all times.

Total Family Participation

This option keeps children with their parents for the entire house-church gathering. The teaching and worship are geared to the children, and families learn together. These house churches might have a supplemental ministry for parents, such as an occasional men's breakfast, ladies' outing or small-group meetings during the week.

Those who use this option fully integrate children and
teens into the house-church meetings, giving them the opportunity to contribute at each and every gathering. This kind of
multigenerational approach, where younger generations are
given the chance to teach older ones, works well in a house-
church setting. We've said it before and we'll say it again: The
Lord values children. They can and should take an active role
in house-church life because they are an equal and important
part of the spiritual family.

When children and adults are together, children understand
that they are not given second-class status or segregated from
the adult group. Instead, they are welcomed! Incorporating children is also beneficial because they can see their parents and
other adults in authentic, spiritual relationships. Here is how
one house church makes their meetings family-oriented, keeping the children with them the entire time:

> All the kids in our group stay with us. We eat a meal
> together, take communion together, sing together—the
> kids often request their favorite songs. After singing,
> one family does an activity they have prepared that
> often is a "hands-on" activity or game that offers a godly
> message or teaching for the kids. The adults join the
> kids in this activity (singles and teens, too!). Afterwards,
> when individuals begin to share in the meeting, the kids
> are given the chance to read any Bible passages that we
> discuss. Otherwise, the young ones can draw or color
> while they remain in the room with us, sitting on the
> couch, snuggled with a parent, sprawled on the living
> room floor. Of course, much of the discussion goes over
> their heads! They're kids! But they are with us through-
> out most of our time together, and are permitted to be
> kids. One of the families has a pool in back and some-

times we hold our gathering on their back patio and let the kids swim and have fun together. Now here's the thing: they love our times of fellowship, and the children all feel like they are extended family with one another—brothers and sisters. They look forward to any time we get together with any of the other families and have little difficulty communicating with either adults or other kids. When visiting families come, their children are welcomed without reservation.[3]

Other Options

Another option some parents prefer is to hire their own babysitter for their younger children while they attend house-church gatherings. This gives the parents a "night out." They can receive uninterrupted ministry and learn to minister to others while their children are cared for at home. This method is more common in some parts of Europe.

Some homogeneous house churches of senior citizens, youth, singles or married couples without children may not even have a children's ministry or focus. Couples with children probably should not get involved in a homogenous house church of this type.

Every house church will have their own unique way of incorporating children into the life of the church. One thing that is not unique about incorporating children in house churches is that flexibility and creativity are the keys.

Integrated Through Relationship

No matter which option you choose, children participating in house churches have the opportunity to see the Holy Spirit at work in real-life situations as families meet together as the Church—and children can even play a role in the Holy Spirit's work!

The Lord honors the prayers of children (see 1 Cor. 2:4-5). They can demonstrate the Holy Spirit's power just as adults can. Encourage children to lay their hands on those who are sick and to pray for healing. Include them in creative times of prayer for the nations. Believe and pray with them for their friends to come to Jesus. Make prayer times interactive. Kids will find this type of prayer to be natural, and the adults may enjoy prayer for the first time!

Creativity and flexibility are the keys to providing fellowship for kids who want a real walk with God. House churches might consider investing in a few good children's activity resources. The book *Biblical Foundations for Children* by Jane Nicholas, for example, teaches children basic Christian principles and is ideal for children in house churches.[4]

Some activities we suggest for the children's group leader include working with the children on a project for a missionary, planning special performances (dances, puppet shows, skits) and presenting them at a special event or retirement community, and getting involved in a work project (like cleaning cars or mowing lawns) for shut-ins. The sky is the limit for involving children and young teens in house-church activities!

Notes

1. Don Trotter, quoted in Steve Atkerson, *Ekklesia: To the Roots of Biblical House Church Life* (Atlanta, GA: New Testament Restoration Foundation, 2003), p. 87.
2. Felicity Dale, ed., *Getting Started* (Austin, TX: House2House, 2003), pp. 146-148.
3. Posted by Lisa C. from Florida, Web Forum, www.Housechurch.org, 2006.
4. Jane Nicholas, *Biblical Foundations for Children* (Lititz, PA: House to House Publications, 1999).

CHAPTER 11

GUESS WHO'S LEADING THE WAY?

The center of evangelical Christianity, which was born in England and nurtured in the United States, is shifting away from the West. Most evangelicals now live in China, South Korea, India, Africa and Latin America.

"In unpredictable places and unpredictable times, you get real savvy leaders," said Mark Noll, a professor of history at Wheaton College. "I suspect that in Beijing, Nairobi or Cape Town, things will be very well along with innovation before Philadelphia, Chicago or London is aware of it. Almost everything that's significant takes place below the radar screen."[1] "Below the radar screen" means that we Western followers of Jesus have little awareness of the massive move of God taking place in the developing world.

In other words, as the vibrancy of evangelicalism seems to be waning in the West, many in the East and global South have picked up the banner and are moving forward with it. Foremost among these are house churches, thriving in nations outside our Western culture. These non-Western brothers and sisters in Christ are setting the standard for us here in America and in Europe.

China

The revival in China today, for example, is considered the largest spiritual harvest since the book of Acts. This revival was fueled by the severe persecution of Christians during the Cultural Revolution. Today, an estimated 35,000 Chinese become Christians every day through various house-church movements that have sprung up throughout their nation. There are over 100 million believers in these unregistered house churches in China.[2]

The Chinese Church has gone "underground" in house churches out of necessity. They do not register their churches with the government because to do so would mean waiting until their children are 18 years of age before teaching them about Christ. Because of the governmental restrictions they face, Chinese Christians are committed to following the biblical pattern of house church.

In light of these hardships, God has poured out His grace on the Chinese Church. This underground church is probably experiencing the greatest move of God in history since Pentecost, and it is all happening in and through house churches. The Chinese Church is the most strategically organized church in the world, and it is all networked through house churches.

A few years ago, I (Larry) had the opportunity to minister to 80 of the key leaders of the underground church movements in China. It was a life-changing experience for me. Meeting these humble men and women of God deeply moved me. I know one thing for sure: They taught me far more than I could ever teach them. Ninety-five percent of these leaders—many of whom had traveled for days by train to get to the secluded leadership training seminar—had been imprisoned for their faith. One elderly leader had been released only four days before. Another precious man of God, who sat at my breakfast table, humbly told me about his leadership of 10 million house-church members through the network he oversees. I sat in amazement! It was as if I was in another world.

I also met a group of women who oversee house-church leaders, one of whom was responsible for 400,000 believers involved in her network. They told stories of how they were raped in prison yet stayed true to the Lord and continued to birth house churches to accommodate the new believers coming to Christ all over their nation.

During my time in China, I was asked to teach on the biblical truth of becoming spiritual fathers and mothers. After many of the sessions I taught, these humble men and women of God stood, prayed and repented. They repented because they felt that they were so caught up in the work of God that they were not focusing enough on His workers. It was a humbling experience for me. This is a great lesson for all of us to learn. We can become so caught up in God's work—including the starting of new house churches—that we lose sight of our call from the Lord to be spiritual fathers and mothers to the next generation.

There is one last thing that I learned from the Chinese during my visit, which is applicable to the house-church movement in the U.S. today: When I asked the Chinese leadership if the people in their house churches tithed, they said yes. When I asked them if the house-church pastors received support from the tithe, they smiled and informed me that only those individuals who were willing to be sent out as missionaries or apostolic leaders to other parts of China received any financial support. Only when they have the responsibility to oversee other house-church leaders are leaders supported financially. This is also true of most house-church leaders in North America—most must either own a business or work another job to support themselves and their families. House-church leaders around the world, then, are "tent-makers" like Aquila and Priscilla who had a church in their home (see Rom. 16:3-5; 1 Cor. 16:19).

The Chinese Vision to Send Missionaries

The Chinese Church has a long-reaching vision to train 100,000 missionaries in their own country and send them out to take the good news of Christ to millions in spiritual darkness across Asia. The plan is called "Back to Jerusalem" because these church-planting missionaries will make their way west

toward Jerusalem by the ancient Silk Road (which has connected the Middle East with the Far East for 6,000 years) on a mission journey to unreached people groups, particularly Muslims.

The missionaries will plant churches as they take three main
routes through the final frontiers of the least evangelized nations
in the world. The first two routes are meant to evangelize mostly through Muslim countries, while the third route will evangelize through the center of the Buddhist and Hindu world:

> The first missionaries are already on their way. Many
> more are preparing themselves for the Great Task, and
> will soon follow the others. They are learning different
> languages, for example Arabic and English. They are also
> being educated in learning the manners and culture of
> the countries they will enter.[3]

There has already been significant revival in Nepal, as well
as in various parts of Vietnam and India. The churches that the
Chinese have founded in these three countries serve as bases for
the further planting of churches:

> The Chinese know that it is of no avail to come to these
> countries with words only. They must come in power as
> well, the power of the Gospel—with signs and wonders
> to convince the people that there is a living and real
> God whom they can serve.[4]

Future Strategy of the Chinese Church

The Chinese house-church movement has already committed to
the Lord that if freed from Communism in the future, the
Church will build no buildings. They want to keep their method
of training and sending intact. Rather than concentrating on
constructing buildings, they want to focus on building people.

They seek to accomplish this by:

1. Not allowing any "pastor" to stay in one place for a long period of time, since this can create a dependency on leadership to do the evangelism and church planting that all believers should be doing;

2. Continuing their commitment to build and model teamwork; and

3. Keeping a tabernacle mentality rather than a temple mentality—like the Israelites wandering in the desert, they will move when the cloud moves.

Latin America, India, Cambodia

Several years ago, there was a paradigm shift in the way the Southern Baptist Mission Board approached missions. The board decided to plant churches the way the book of Acts described it: by training and releasing. The mission board developed a church-planting strategy that they defined as *a rapid and exponential increase of indigenous churches planting churches within a given people group or population segment.*

In Latin America, church planters began by becoming spiritual fathers and mothers who trained and released their spiritual sons and daughters to become new house-church planters. In 1989, there were 129 churches in one area of Latin America. Nine years later, the number had grown exponentially to 1,918! One factor that fueled the growth of these house-church networks was the severe economic crisis in Latin America during the early 1990s. Through that time, church members were prevented from traveling long distances to their church buildings, so they "moved their meetings into homes and found that growth greatly accelerated."[5]

India began in 1989 with 28 churches and grew to 2,000 over the course of those same nine years. The Baptists implemented a plan for growth that included sending disciples out two by two, just as Jesus did in Luke 10. They found "men of peace" in targeted villages, moved in with them and began to disciple their families. "As these initial converts came to faith, they led their families to the Lord, baptized them and forged them into the nucleus of new churches in each village."[6]

Similar results were encountered in Cambodia, a country with an infrastructure that lay in shambles due to wars and dictatorships. In the same 9 years, 6 Cambodian churches grew into 194 churches, the majority of which were networked house churches. As the church-planting movement unfolded, the momentum burned from within:

> Local leaders expressed their own vision for planting churches in every district and within each ethnic community. As they acquired training and encouragement, the primary church planters were the church members themselves, rather than missionaries or professional church planters. The coordinator later observed that "churches planted by other churches are reproducible, but those started by funded church planters are not (with few exceptions)."[7]

Muslim Countries

The largest church-planting movement among Muslims is currently unfolding in central Asia. This movement began with two young men: Sharif and his friend Bilal.

In 1983, a missionary befriended Sharif and through that relationship, Sharif became a Christian. Consequently, Sharif's family disowned him, and he was often beaten by members of his community. Things started to change in 1991, however, when Sharif led his friend Bilal to the Lord and the two were baptized. The following year, the two men led their first Muslim family to Christ and started the first house church in their Islamic community. Over the next decade, they saw nearly 4,000 churches planted and more than 150,000 Muslims come to faith in Christ.[8]

The Heart of Church-Planting Success

House-church planting movements are proliferating worldwide. "The vast majority of the churches continue to be small, reproducible simple churches of 10-30 members meeting in homes or storefronts."[9] This kind of multiplication is a phenomenon that is becoming more and more commonplace.

> A missionary strategist assigned to a North Indian people group found just 28 churches among them in 1989. By the year 2000, a church planting movement had erupted catapulting the number of churches to more than 4,500 with an estimated 300,000 baptized believers.
>
> In Southeast Asia, a missionary strategist began working with three small house churches of 85 members in 1993. Just seven years later, membership had swollen to more than 90,000 baptized believers worshiping in 920 churches.[10]

The Baptists were among those who realized that house churches are at the heart of successful church-planting movements. This is for three reasons:

1. *House churches reproduce rapidly.* Therefore, a church-planting movement based on house churches has rapid increases in new church starts.

2. *House churches increase by multiplication.* Multiplicative increase is only possible when an existing church—rather than professional church planters or missionaries—start new churches. Expansion becomes exponential.

3. *House churches are indigenous.* This means that they multiply from within rather than without. This is not to say that the gospel is able to spring up spontaneously within a people group. The gospel nearly always enters a people group from the outside—this is the task of the cross-cultural church planter. But in a church-planting movement, the initiative and drive come from within the indigenous people group rather than from those on the outside. Indigenous people already have established relationships with others in their community and house churches are *all about* relationships, so house churches are a natural fit in close-knit populations.

What About the West?

Baptist church-planting movements are seeing success in largely non-Western cultures. David Garrison, author of *Church Planting Movements,* speaks out about why he believes we have not yet seen huge movements in the Western world, and why we need them:

> One of the common characteristics that we've seen of church planting movements is persecution, and in many open democracies, you don't have that. Persecution often creates a climate of urgent need in response to Christ. One Western church planting movement that we did see was in Amsterdam among immigrants, refugees

who came into the area. They were extremely responsive and began reproducing churches at a rapid clip.

There is an awful lot to commend house churches in the United States. There are quantifiable realities, such as the cost of church buildings, the exploding population, the increase in urbanization and the increasing cost of property in the cities. There is no way we can build enough church buildings. It becomes a question of stewardship. Can you justify putting 20-30 million dollars into building a church just so that you can add another 1,000 people to a church that already has a couple of thousand people? I am concerned about the 80+ million unchurched Americans. I'm not convinced that our existing structures will draw them in. The house church movement has the potential to do that.[11]

We agree with Garrison's assessment of the importance of house churches in a church-planting movement in Western culture. It is in our best interest in North America and other Western cultures to begin thinking in terms of initiating whole movements, not just one house church. That means a change of strategy or, perhaps even more fundamental, a change of paradigm about how to do church. There is a great need to move our emphasis and resources toward small, simple, easily reproducible churches that can spontaneously multiply into a church-planting movement. Of course, this will not happen without the Holy Spirit breathing on our efforts. In Acts 13, when Barnabas and Saul were sent out of the church in Antioch, they started a church-planting *movement*. Chapters 13 through 15 in the book of Acts tell the story of this new movement and how it mushroomed from house to house nearly everywhere they went. *Lord, grant us the grace to experience the same today.*

Notes

1. Paul Nussbaum, "The Tide Is Turning," Lancaster New Era, 2006.
2. Geoff Waugh, "Astounding Church Growth," *Renewal Journal*, vol. 93, no. 2, pp. 47-57. http://www.pastornet.net.au/renewal/journal2/waugh.html (accessed January 2007). Barbara Nield, "China's House Churches," *Renewal Journal*, vol. 94, no. 1, pp. 48-60. http://www.pastornet.net.au/renewal/journal3/neild.html (accessed January 2007).
3. Haavald Slaatten, *The Heavenly Man* (Ontario, Canada: Guardian Books, 2000), p. 128.
4. Ibid., p. 129.
5. David Garrison, *Church Planting Movements* (Richmond, VA: International Mission Board of the Southern Baptist Convention, 1999), p. 14.
6. Ibid., p. 23.
7. Ibid., p. 30.
8. David Garrison, *Church Planting Movements* (Bangalore, India: WIGTake Resources, 2004), p. 115.
9. David Garrison, *Church Planting Movements* (Richmond, VA: International Mission Board of the Southern Baptist Convention, 1999), p. 35.
10. Ibid., p. 17.
11. "A Telephone Interview with David Garrison," *House2House Magazine*, issue 2, p. 9.

CHAPTER 12

HOUSE CHURCHES IN NORTH AMERICA

I was shocked to discover how big our house-church community in North America really is. Briefly stated, we're right about halfway between the Catholic Church and the Southern Baptist Convention," said Jim Rutz.

Rutz was referring to the numbers that George Barna, the leading U.S. church pollster revealed in his new book, *Revolution*. Barna's statistics are based on a four-month scientific survey of 5,013 adults categorized by various indicators, including 663 blacks, 631 Hispanics, 676 liberals and 1,608 conservatives. People may not agree with Barna's conclusions and theories, but the numbers themselves are solid. The Barna Group employs all the professional safeguards to ensure tight results—in this case, a sampling error of ±1.8 percent. Here are five ways of stating the results:

1. In a typical week, 9 percent of U.S. adults attend a house church.
2. In absolute numbers, that 9 percent equals roughly 20 million people.
3. In a typical month, about 43 million U.S. adults attend a house church.
4. All told, 70 million U.S. adults have at least experimented with participation in a house church.
5. Focusing *only* on those who attend some kind of church (which I recall is about 43 percent of us), 74

percent of them attend only a traditional church, 19
percent attend both a traditional and a house church
and 5 percent are hardcore house-church folks.[1]

This study counted only attendance at house churches,
not small groups (or cells) that are part of a traditional church.
Barna's study makes it clear that simple house churches are
not only growing exponentially in places like China, India and
Latin America. During the past few years, thousands of new
house churches—often networking together—have sprung up
throughout North America. House-church networks have
emerged in Denver, Dallas, Austin, Cincinnati, San Francisco
and Portland—and that's just the tip of the iceberg.

The study by The Barna Group shows that "millions of
adults are trying out new forms of spiritual community and
worship, with many abandoning the traditional forms alto-
gether." If this trend continues over the next two decades, it will
"substantially reduce the share of adults who call a conventional church their primary spiritual community."[2]

Mike Steele, a simple church leader from Colorado, has
been connected with this movement of God for almost a decade.
The message of a "simple life in Christ" has spawned the
growth of simple church networks throughout the U.S. and
Canada. Mike believes that God is stirring the Body of Christ
in the West in much the same way as He has been stirring the
Body in the non-Western settings. What started with people
planting churches in homes has continued to mature into a
movement where people see church as people living a "daily
lifestyle of Christ-likeness" in the midst of their friends and
family. Rather than focusing just on a meeting, the meeting is
a supplement to the life that house-church members live
together in Jesus. Here's how Mike describes the movements
he's seeing:

In Las Vegas, Nevada, a group of seasoned veterans (most are now in their early to mid-thirties!) have weathered a decade of walking with the Lord in the crucible of community. In the heart of "sin city," they share life with bar waitresses, card dealers and hotel employees in their homes and communities. They have created an atmosphere of acceptance and healing. Many come and participate even before they come to know the Lord. For them, this is the first time they have experienced the love of Christ in tangible ways.

In nearby Los Angeles, I connected with a wonderful group of sojourners who carry the same heart and passion to see Christ's kingdom bursting forth. They have focused on discipleship and meetings in small groups for intimate fellowship. Many who are responding to this approach are in their 20s and come from fractured backgrounds. Others are reaching into various alternate lifestyle communities.

They use a simple, yet intimate discipleship process called LTGs. These "Life Transformation Groups" are made up of three people who read 30 chapters of scripture a week, confess their sins for cleansing and healing, and pray for a friend to join them. As a fourth joins they begin a new group. These meetings are valuable supports to the life they live out daily in their communities and spheres of influence. Thousands of these groups have sprung up around the world in recent years.

Not all networks of these new models of church are as exotic as those cited above. But from California to Maryland, from Washington to Florida, I am receiving calls and emails from traditional pastors and leaders seeking help in transitioning into ways of living out the "life of Christ" in the midst of their communities. We are excited about the shift to reproduction flowing out of healthy relationships and deep discipleship. Deep and abiding relationships lead to trust and the ability to hear the Lord together and follow His lead.[3]

DAWN Ministries is a saturation church-planting movement that has a vision for "seeing vibrant, witnessing gatherings established in the midst of every small group of people in every neighborhood and community amongst every class, kind and condition of mankind in every nation on earth." They list a number of house-church networks on their North American website (www.dawnministries.org). Here are several:

- Vineyard Central in Cincinnati has transitioned from a traditional Vineyard church into an expanding network of house churches. In the last year they doubled in size from 10 to 20 micro-churches, each networked with the others.

- The Friends Church in the Northwest is also noted on the DAWN website and now has 20 to 25 organic churches all over the Pacific Northwest.

- In the Dallas area, there is an emerging network of Southern Baptist micro-churches, and the Southern Baptists along the Front Range in Colorado have approximately 30 house churches.

- In California, Jonathan Campbell and his wife, Jennifer, lead a flourishing network that features house churches in Riverside, Los Angeles, Pasadena, Santa Cruz, San Diego, San Jose and San Francisco. They also have house churches in Orlando, Florida; Boise, Idaho; and Seattle and Kitsap County, Washington.

The list goes on and on—DAWN mentions house churches in Mesa and Phoenix, Arizona; in Salt Lake City, Utah; in urban Columbus, Ohio; and more![4]

Internet Fuels Interest

With the dawn of the Internet, the house-church movement received a huge boost. If you look today at the number of home-church websites on the Internet, it's phenomenal. In ever-increasing and innovative ways, the Internet provides opportunities to reach certain groups of people that would never have been reached by traditional churches. House churches owe the Internet credit for much of their exchange of information.

John White, a Denver-based house-church leader, agrees that the Internet has facilitated the more recent rise of home churches. White says that when he quit his job as a Presbyterian minister to start a home church eight years ago, it was difficult to find anyone who would join up with him. Now he has an e-mail list of more than 800 people nationwide who receive his posts about practical issues of home churching. "With more access to religious information online, people are realizing they don't have to rely on a pastor with an advanced degree to lead them . . . this is in keeping with God's plan to have a kingdom of priests, in which everyone participates in his or her religious life," White says.[5]

Churches Are Networking

Frontline Ministries, led by John and Kathy Johnson, is a church plant of the cell-based Indianapolis Christian Fellowship. Both Frontline Ministries and Indianapolis Christian Fellowship are part of DOVE Christian Fellowship International's family of churches. John and Kathy report that they have various kinds of homogeneous groups in their network: college age groups, young families groups and senior groups. John describes one house church of mostly young families as "little kids in the middle of the floor surrounded by adults who corral them in. It sometimes seems like a zoo, at least to an empty nester like myself. As much as I love this group, I normally leave with a small twitch in my eye! But, these families intertwine their lives and always have room for another single mom or young family."

House churches in the network get together to serve at a local soup kitchen and the Ronald McDonald House, hold neighborhood and family outreaches, and support needy families in their city.

Mark and Sarah Rife lead Elevate, a student church in Hilo, Hawaii. Elevate is part of the All Nations network of churches, connected by relationship and shared values and vision. Small-group communities form the core of Elevate and function like house churches where discipleship, outreach and community happen. Mark and the rest of the team are very cognizant of setting the DNA in the life-blood of their movement. I (Floyd) have appreciated the emphasis that Mark and Sarah have put on missional church as well as the ways they are committed to raising up a band of leaders who have a passion to reach their friends and neighbors and impact the nations.

House of Service in Post Falls, Idaho, is a house church led by Bruce and Alice Preston. They maintain ties with their cell-based sending church, River City Network, through monthly joint celebrations. This house church of 22 people has a vision for outreach and multiplication and to see everyone come into their calling and gifts that God has given them.

The Boiler Room in Kansas City is an alternative church that is closely tied to the 24-7 prayer movement. It is led by a team of twenty-somethings including Adam Cox, Julie Cox, Nathan and Marissa Church, and David and Molly Blackwell.

Consisting of mostly 18- to 35-year-olds, they live out the simple values of Christ and His message to the world in a missional community built around friendship, prayer and mission. This fledgling group, currently about 80 to 90 strong, meets on the second floor of an art gallery loft for weekly celebrations and in small groups in one another's homes. They seek to engage the culture of their city by helping inner-city children and battered women, resettling refugees, and conducting 24-7 prayer vigils on the local university campus.

Luis and Pamela Perez serve a growing and vital network of micro-churches in the greater Rochester, New York, region. Perez transitioned from 16 years of serving on the pastoral staff of a local mega-church because he saw the need for a different strategy to reach the pre-churched and spiritually homeless. Sixteen months after starting their first micro-church, they had a total of 10 house churches, whose mission is to "facilitate the reality of Jesus Christ right where people live, play and work— void of the religious mentality that means nothing to those who haven't met Jesus yet, and often serves as a barrier to true engagement with the world around us by believers."

Gates of Praise, Wayne Kaufman's house-church network in Lancaster County, Pennsylvania, has a vision to "change the world for Jesus one house at a time." Wayne says, "Our mission is to express the fullness of Christ through individual house churches in community with a network of house churches, whose purpose is to evangelize the world, make disciples of all nations by equipping and training healthy servant leaders, and to build up and plant new house churches."

The Underground is a house-church network of communities that grew out of InterVarsity's student ministry in Tampa, Florida. Led by Brian Sanders and a core group of friends that have made long-term commitments to each other, The Underground is passionate about prayer and justice—so passionate that Brian and his house church are *all* going to trans-plant for a year to the Philippines to learn by serving among the poor.

The Lancaster Micro-Church Network (LMCN), which Mike Stolzfus oversees in Lancaster County, Pennsylvania, is a network of church networks. In the greater Lancaster area, a micro-church network called The Net was birthed in 2004, and another micro-church network, The Circle Community, was launched in 2006. Both networks have found a home with the LMCN where they share resources, common values and a common vision to plant new house churches.

The Same Thing All Over the World!

About 10 years after planting a new church, I (Larry) received a phone call from Ralph Neighbour's office, inviting me to meet him at a cell-group seminar in New Jersey where he was speak-ing. I knew Ralph from his book *Where Do We Go from Here?*, which the Lord had used to open the hearts of thousands worldwide to the cell-group movement.

"Tell me your story," Ralph said when we met in New Jersey. As I told him about how our church started with one cell group and grew to over 2,300 people all participating in home groups, tears began to stream down his face. "The Lord is doing the same thing all over the world," Ralph exclaimed. "People who have never met, who have never heard of one another, are using the same terminology because the Lord is doing the same thing through them in many parts of the world. This is truly the Lord."

As Floyd and I travel week after week, we continue to hear the same thing. God is continuing to pour out His Spirit on ordinary people, changing their very lifestyles as they meet together in simple, biblically based churches. People no longer perceive a conflict between house churches in North America and the traditional church. In fact, noted leaders like Rick Warren have recently come out in favor of house churches. Saddleback Church is sending their members out as "missionaries" to start house-church networks.[6]

We have both served as senior pastors of mega-churches and we have served in community churches of different sizes and flavors—and these types of church will continue to have their place in North America. But today, Floyd and I both oversee international church movements (DOVE Christian Fellowship International and All Nations, respectively). Both of us have a vision for these networks to include house-church networks. For example, the All Nations church planting strategy is based on the concept of small, simple, easily reproducible house churches as we seek to reach Hindus, Muslims, Buddhists and other neglected people groups with the good news of Jesus' love.

The house-church movement is no longer a fringe movement in North America or the world. In fact, many church families and denominations throughout the world are involved in the house-church movement. House churches are alive and well and growing, in our nation and in many other nations. House churches, simple churches or micro-churches are meeting the needs of many North Americans as they seek new forms of spiritual community and worship.

To learn more about the amazing impact that church-planting movements are having, we recommend that you read David Garrison's outstanding book *Church Planting Movements*. The greatest growth in the world is taking place—in terms of quality and quantity—in church-planting movements that emphasize *dreaming big* and *building small*.

Notes

1. Jim Rutz, "A Major Announcement about House Churches," WorldNetDaily, June 27, 2006. http://www.worldnetdaily.com/news/article.asp?ARTICLE_ID=50802 (accessed December 2006).

2. The Barna Group, "House Church Involvement Is Growing," June 19, 2006. http://www.barna.org/FlexPage.aspx?Page=BarnaUpdateNarrow&BarnaUpdateID=241 (accessed December 2006).

3. Mike Steele, "Simple Church Growth in North America 2006 Overview," August 2006.

4. DAWN Ministries, www.dawnministries.org.

5. Michael Alison Chandler and Arianne Aryanpur, "Going to Church by Staying at Home," *The Washington Post*, Sunday, June 4, 2006, p. A-12.

6. Jim Rutz, "A Major Announcement About House Churches," WorldNetDaily, June 27, 2006. http://www.worldnetdaily.com/news/article.asp?ARTICLE_ID =50802 (accessed December 2006).

CHAPTER 13

WHAT ABOUT LEADERSHIP?

All around us, in every sector of society, there are leaders. In the political realm, nations are led by presidents and prime ministers. Businesses have presidents and CEOs. Sports teams have captains. The role of these leaders is to set the direction of the nation, organization or team that they lead, and they have authority to make key and strategic decisions.

In the Bible, too, we see examples of people to whom God chooses to provide leadership. While everyone in the Church is called to be a servant leader, not everyone possesses the gifts and abilities to lead a church community or network. There are examples in the Bible of men and women to whom God gave special tasks of leadership. Moses, for example, was appointed to lead the people of Israel out of slavery in Egypt and into the land God had set aside for them. God used Moses in this pursuit so that His people would know Him and be a blessing to the other peoples of the earth. At the end of Moses' life, his leadership position transferred to Joshua. When Joshua gained the position of leadership, God assured Joshua that He would be present with him, just as He had been with Moses (see Josh. 1:1-9).

David was also a leader chosen by God. God chose David to be king of Israel in a time of turmoil in the nation's history. Though David made mistakes, and in some instances sinned grievously, he was a brilliant general and leader for his people. Deborah is another example of a great leader in the Bible. Her courage in facing the enemies of her people and her defiance of those who had lost their integrity are examples every leader should heed.

Similarly, we see examples of men and women of God throughout Church history who have led a church or movement to accomplish God's purposes. In the sixth century, Patrick and Columbanus led a movement of Celtic missionaries to the tribal nations of Europe. In the sixteenth century, Luther led the Church to rediscover the crucial fact that we are made right in God's eyes by faith in the work of Christ, not by our own efforts. In the 1700s, John Wesley led an evangelistic and church-planting movement that transformed England. In the nineteenth century, Hudson Taylor led a new missionary force that went to places that in his day were completely unreached with the message of Christ's love.

Today, however, people—particularly those in house churches—are questioning the concept of leadership for a variety of reasons. Some have experienced abusive, controlling leadership; those who have been affected by such leadership want nothing to do with it, and with good reason. These people might point to passages in Scripture such as Matthew 20:20 where Jesus specifically and in strong language tells His followers that they should not "lord it over people."

Others feel that the very nature of house church—where the numbers of people attending are small compared to more traditional congregations—does away with the need for a leader. They feel that the group can make all decisions together. Some go so far as to say that looking to leaders to make decisions aligns itself with contemporary society and unbiblical mores. Still others take the truth that in the new covenant, there is no longer a special class of persons set aside to lead (like the priests in the Old Testament). These people believe (rightly, in our view) that the New Testament teaches that we are all priests and ministers (see 1 Pet. 2:9)—only they interpret this to mean (wrongly, in our view) that there should be no leaders.

Do House Churches Need Leaders?

Perhaps we have hit upon one of the most controversial aspects of house church. Should we have leaders? To this question, we make a number of responses.

First, the Scriptures make it clear that God places leaders in the Church. First Peter 2:13 urges us to submit ourselves to every authority "instituted" among men. The implication of the Greek word "instituted" or "built" is that God Himself initiates the roles of leaders in the Church. That does not imply that God blesses the ways that ungodly people govern but simply that God ordained the function of leadership.[1]

Second, we see leadership exercised throughout the Scriptures. We have cited some Old Testament examples in this chapter, but leadership continues beyond the Old Testament through the life and ministry of Jesus, into the era of the New Covenant and the Early Church. The Lord Jesus Himself clearly led a small group of men and exemplified all the characteristics of a *great* leader. He had vision, strategy and a plan to train and release His followers to carry on His work after He was gone (see John 10:10). He not only released them while on the earth (see Luke 10), but He also prepared them to go on and do even greater things than He had done (see John 14:12). *That's* leadership.

New Testament Leadership

The New Testament teaches us a number of vital truths concerning leadership:

- It shows us examples of leaders appointing leaders and urges *us* to appoint leaders in a similar way;
- It shows ordinary people taking leadership initiative;
- It provides guidelines and standards so that we know who may lead;

- It outlines the function and responsibilities of a leader;
- It helps us determine how decisions can be made in a godly way; and
- It shows us the heart and spirit required of those who lead (see Acts 14:23; 15:1; 16:14; 1 Cor. 16:16; 1 Tim. 5:17,19; 3:1-2; Titus 1:5,7; 2:15; 1 Pet. 5:1; 2 Pet. 2:10).

In the first-century Church, every follower of Jesus could be filled with the Holy Sprit and minister to others. In Acts 14:21, we read of Paul and Barnabas returning to Lystra, Iconium and Antioch to strengthen and encourage the believers. In verse 23, we read that "Paul and Barnabas appointed elders in each church and, with prayer and fasting, committed them to the Lord, in whom they had put their trust." The New Testament church clearly had leaders who exercised spiritual authority.

The practice of exercising spiritual authority is reinforced in Paul's letter to Titus, in which he wrote, "The reason I left you in Crete was that you might straighten out what was left unfinished and appoint elders in every town, as I directed you" (Titus 1:5). In fact, this passage of Scripture goes on to enumerate the qualifying characteristics of spiritual leaders in the Church so that we can know the kinds of people to appoint—namely those with godly character and proven maturity.[2] Throughout Paul's letters, both in narrative and in clear teaching, the responsibilities of leaders are made clear. We believe those responsibilities are threefold: to guard, to govern and to guide (teach).

Leaders Are to Guard and Protect

When addressing the Ephesian elders, Paul said, "Keep watch over yourselves and all the flock of which the Holy Sprit has made you overseers. Be shepherds of the church of God, which he bought with his own blood. I know that after I leave, savage wolves will come in among you and will not spare the flock. Even from your own number men will arise and distort the truth in order to draw away disciples after them. So be on your guard!" (Acts 20:28,31).

Leaders Are to Govern
Leaders are responsible to manage the church's resources and direct the church's decisions (see 1 Tim. 3:4-5). Though church government can take many forms, the bottom line is that God holds leaders responsible for the decisions made by a local church. Wise leaders include those who are affected by their choices in the decision-making process, but they are the ones ultimately responsible for the decisions made.

Leaders Are to Guide Through Teaching
This includes discipling others to follow Jesus and encouraging the hearts of the believers. When necessary, leaders are also called to bring correction (see 2 Tim. 4:2). Teaching the Bible in house church often takes the form of leading a Bible discussion. In small groups, like those in a house church, a well-led discussion is often a more powerful way for the Bible to speak to people's hearts than for one person to do all the talking.

One Leader—or a Team?

One of the things we notice in many of the Scripture passages we have cited is that leadership is referred to in the plural. It is "elders" (plural) who should be appointed, not just one "elder" (singular). We see the Early Church concept of team leadership as a good example for us today, and believe it should be taught and practiced.

While there were teams of people practicing leadership in the churches in the book of Acts, however, there was always one person who was the primary leader of the team. An Old Testament example of this dynamic is Miriam, Aaron and Moses working together as a team. Moses was the leader of the three, and when Miriam claimed to have the same leadership role as her brother Moses, she contracted leprosy (see Num. 12)!

In Acts 15, we see the apostles and elders meeting in council, where everyone contributed to the debate. Eventually, however, it was James who stood up and gave the verdict. He was the primary leader of all the leadership in Jerusalem.

In order for a team to be effective and for a leader to lead effectively, we believe that one person needs to be given freedom to lead and make decisions for the leadership group.[3]

Leadership Today

But what of the fact that we live in a postmodern world and that house churches are small in number? Do these factors affect leadership? Yes, we believe they do—but these issues bring us to matters of style, spiritual maturity and group dynamics rather than the fundamental question of whether leadership is needed or not.

There are churches and cultures that function well without recognized leaders and there are others that do not. In our experience, a team without a designated leader can function well if all the members are mature, but often a leaderless team hinders what God wants to do in a church—and in some cases, causes the church to self-destruct. We believe biblical principles of leadership apply to every culture and bring the greatest blessing when practiced.

Of course, in a small group, everyone will be more involved in giving decision-making input, which is just not possible in a congregation of 100 or more! Group participation, which we wholeheartedly recommend, can encourage people to grow in leadership and is one of the many advantages of house church. At the end of the day, however, there still needs to be someone serving as a spiritual mom or dad in the spiritual family, discerning from God and watching over the flock. The biblical principles of leadership are the same (protecting, governing, teaching), regardless of the size or prevailing culture of a group—only the outworking of those principles will vary.

In the Early Church, there were always spiritual leaders. If the house church did not yet have leaders, we find in the New Testament that the new believers looked to Paul or to the apostles for leadership until local leaders were appointed. In his book *Cell Groups and House Churches—What History Teaches Us,* Peter Bunton's study of church history shows that groups that were most successful and had the farthest-reaching impact were those where clear leadership and leadership training were in place.[4] The Church's history and current experience support the scriptural principles of leadership detailed above. Our perspective is simply this: The church is a family, and families need parents.

When a group today says they have no need for leaders, it is wise to listen closely, because the one who says this the loudest is usually the leader—though he or she may not want to admit it. When we (Larry and LaVerne) started our first house church more than 25 years ago, we encouraged the believers not to designate one person as a leader, but instead to choose a team that would provide equal leadership. Each house group had two equal leaders, and six equal leaders led the church network.

On the surface, this sounded good and noble. In reality, it was a manifestation of false humility. Under the surface, there was struggle. With six of us leading, one Sunday morning we couldn't even decide who should preach in our meeting. Since none of us were in the clear leadership position, no one preached! It would have been fine for no one to preach if the Lord was truly leading us not to, but since it was by default, it caused confusion and stress in the congregation. Within the first year, our "leaderless" group came to the difficult realization that there was a clear need for leadership among us. Although we continued to believe that team leadership was important, we recognized the need for one person on the team to be the official leader.

Two spiritual leaders from our area agreed to oversee and serve our fledgling group, helping us through difficult times until two from the original six co-leaders were set apart and ordained by a local denomination that was committed to supporting us during those early years. I (Larry) was acknowledged as the primary leader of the leadership team. It was only after leadership was clear that we began to grow.[5]

As we've traveled to many nations, we have found that the philosophy of leaderless groups does not exist in nations that are experiencing revival—only in nations like the United States or other countries where the majority of house churches are made up of believers who have come out of traditional churches. This prevailing, negative view of biblical authority may be because some of these Christians have experienced bad or even abusive leadership—but harmful experiences don't nullify God's plan for His family.

True Leadership—the Heart of a Servant

Let's return to the teaching of Jesus in Matthew 20:20-28. Some would say that Jesus teaches that we do not need leadership because it is something of the world. Let's look at the passage a little more closely to determine what Jesus is really saying:

> Then the mother of Zebedee's sons came to Jesus with her sons and, kneeling down, asked a favor of him.
> "What is it you want?" he asked.

She said, "Grant that one of these two sons of mine may sit at your right and the other at your left in your kingdom."

"You don't know what you are asking," Jesus said to them. "Can you drink the cup I am going to drink?"

"We can," they answered.

Jesus said to them, "You will indeed drink from my cup, but to sit at my right or left is not for me to grant. These places belong to those for whom they have been prepared by my Father."

When the ten heard about this, they were indignant with the two brothers. Jesus called them together and said, "You know that the rulers of the Gentiles lord it over them, and their high officials exercise authority over them. Not so with you. Instead, whoever wants to become great among you must be your servant, and whoever wants to be first must be your slave—just as the Son of Man did not come to be served, but to serve, and to give his life as a ransom for many."

This is the heart of Jesus' teaching on leadership. Some observations by Peter Bunton, who led a house church in England, help us to understand exactly what Jesus is saying in Matthew 20:

The Greek verb *to rule* is *kureio*. Here in Matthew 20:25, we find it used with the prefix *kata*, that is *katakureio* (see also 1 Pet. 3:5). These two occurrences of the verb express something far more forceful than leadership or rulership (*kureio*); rather they talk of something more sinister and unhealthy. It is this kind of leadership with which Jesus denounces in Matthew 20, not leadership in itself. What is this kind of leadership? I believe Acts 19:16 gives us a good indication. This is the only other time that *katakureio* is used. Here it speaks of demonic powers completely controlling and overpowering. With this in mind, it seems to me that, in Matthew 20, Jesus is not saying you should not lead, but that we should not lead in the overpowering, destroying way of the demons, that is in an abusive way. Rather our leadership should be exercised from the position of being a servant, preferring the needs of others and helping them. Jesus continues his teaching here by saying, be like me and do as I do—which includes following his leadership pattern.[6]

We certainly agree with Peter's evaluation of the need for godly, servant-hearted leadership in house churches today.

Abuse of Authority

There are many who have been abused by unhealthy leadership in the Body of Christ. In my book *The Father Heart of God*, I (Floyd) wrote about the abuse of authority that can warp the entire concept of spiritual leadership. God calls church leaders to be spiritual fathers and mothers who tread lightly as they point their spiritual children to Jesus, not dominating authority figures that coerce their children into submission. That does not mean that there is not a time and place for leaders to correct, direct and protect those they lead.

Godly fathers and mothers want to serve others and treat all men and women as their equals. Their actions proceed from an attitude of equality—not authority—because they are more concerned with serving than ruling. The following lists highlight the differences between the two approaches.

Dominating Fathers and Mothers:
1. Function as if they are the source of guidance for people's lives.

2. Emphasize the rights of leaders.
3. Set leaders apart and give them special privileges.
4. Seek to control people's actions.
5. Emphasize the importance of leaders ministering to others.
6. Use rules and laws to control people and force them to conform.

Mothers and Fathers in the Lord:

1. Believe that God is the source of guidance and desire to help other Christians learn to hear His voice.
2. Emphasize the responsibilities of leaders, not their rights.
3. Emphasize those in the Body of Christ serving one another.
4. Encourage people to be dependent upon God.
5. Emphasize the importance of equipping the saints for the work of the ministry.
6. Provide an atmosphere of trust and grace to encourage growth.

Biblical authority is never taken—it is *offered*. It comes from the anointing of God's Spirit and is the sum total of one's character, wisdom, spiritual gifts and servant attitude. Mothers and fathers in the Lord understand these principles about authority. They know the character of the Father, so they are relaxed in their ministry to other people. They have learned to take action as God directs, not just because they are "the leader."[7]

Healthy spiritual fathers and mothers earn the right to speak into their spiritual children's lives, and they do so with the heart of a servant, affirming and encouraging their children in their walk with Christ. Godly spiritual fathers and mothers are also willing to exercise correction if necessary, but always in love. If they confront someone who is disruptive or divisive, they do so out of concern for the welfare of the group, not to prove who has a right to lead.

Leaders are called to be servants. If someone feels called to be a leader, his or her charisma and knowledge of the Bible should not be determining factors. The real key to their leadership ability depends on whether or not they love Jesus, love His people and are willing to serve.

How Can Leaders Be Released?

If we agree that biblical leadership is vitally important, the next question is how exactly leadership happens in a new house-church network.

When we started LMCN in Lancaster County, we expected every house church to have elders. After a few years, however, we found that our expectation was slowing the start of new churches, because becoming an elder was such a big step for new believers to take—the word "elder" simply scared them! So we tried something new.

We started a movement within the movement. Mike, one of the founders of that first house church, started the Net, an elder network that allows micro-churches to start up with leaders who do not sense a call to become elders. We recognized that in Acts 14:23, elders were commissioned for every church, whereas in Titus 1:5, elders were appointed in every city. Some house churches now have elders in each house, modeled after Acts 14:23, while others receive leadership from elders in the Net, modeled after Titus 1:5. We split the finances 50/50, with one-half of the tithes and offerings going to the Net and one-half staying with the house church. And it's working! People are excited about planting churches again!

There are four levels of spiritual leadership that have emerged out of the LMCN:

1. Small-group leaders of one, two or three persons who attend house churches
2. Leaders of house churches
3. Leaders of a network of house churches in one area
4. Apostolic leaders, leading an entire movement of house churches in more than one area

We have learned from experience that some house churches find it very hard to plant new churches without an outside catalyst, so we encourage our micro-church leaders to have "incubator meetings" in which leaders and potential leaders of various house churches come together to pray about strategies for new church plants. Occasionally, these leaders even get away overnight for prayer, fellowship and strategizing. In any case, leaders always leave these meetings and retreats with a new sense of excitement and an increase of faith, and sometimes God shows the way for a new church to be planted by believers from more than one existing house church.

One of the ways I (Floyd) have learned to release new church planters is by gathering potential leaders to do a weekly study in the book of Acts over a period of six to nine weeks. We focus on Paul's church-planting strategies, the values he lived by, and how he responded to opposition and persecution. I did this first on a trip to Central Asia with a group of potential church planters. The results were awesome. Several people on that team are still planting churches today! This process of reaching out to new leaders affirms them and helps remind me of the need to select and coach future church planters continually. I have to be intentional if I'm going to create a leader-friendly environment and a church-planting culture.

Regardless of how you rally potential leaders, once those people are identified and discipled, they must be given an opportunity to put your church's values into practice. We believe that the best opportunities happen in a cell group or house church. The best training a future church planter can ever have is to lead and multiply a cell or simple church. Church planters are gatherers, and by coaching a future church planter through the process of raising up assistant leaders, winning and gathering more people and finally multiplying the group into two growing groups, you show them the core of what church planting is all about. If a person can't do these things, there is very little likelihood that he or she can plant a church.

We have found that the in-the-trenches process described above can never be replaced, but it can be augmented in a six- to nine-month training process. To learn more about the programs we run, please visit our websites at www.dcfi.org, www.startinga housechurch.com, www.all-nations.info and www.floydand sally.org.

The Need for Networks

House churches that are not open to becoming a part of a network usually become stagnant and turn inward rather than looking out to their community and the bigger world. Networking is important for a number of reasons. First, it is for protection. All of us need some kind of oversight in our lives—people who watch out for us and pray for us. The same is true of a small church. Second, it's possible for any of us to fall into pride, sin or wrong doctrine, and being accountable is a good preventive measure to stop such things from happening (and deal with them when they do!). Third, it's unlikely that a small church has all the spiritual gifts God gives to the Body of Christ. House-church networks provide a wonderful opportunity to bring in others who have strong gifts to teach and supplement the life of the church.

Most house-church networks are regional, but not all of them. If you are starting a house church, ask God to give you a vision to reach out to others, and then find ways to network together with those who have the same vision and values. Maybe the Lord is even calling you to start your own house-church network. The desire to connect to other house churches will happen naturally out of the need for a connection to other followers of Jesus. Networking must flow out of relationship—it cannot be forced or contrived.

It is important to know and trust the integrity of the person leading the group and agree with the values, beliefs and practices of the group before committing yourself to a house church or house-church network. Remember that not all house churches or networks are the same! Some networks are small, with only a few house churches involved, while others are much larger, with teams of apostolic leaders providing encouragement, oversight and spiritual protection. And though some house churches are healthy, others are unproductive, reactionary and exclusive. Do not be too quick to commit to a network—let it happen relationally. The Lord's timing is important.

True Apostolic Leaders Faithfully Serve

Most small house churches can easily become isolated if they are not part of something larger. Through our experience, we've come to believe that the preferable network is an apostolic movement of house churches. (By *apostolic* we mean a movement that is focused on reaching the unchurched and which is led by someone with pioneering, visionary gifts.) All the house churches in the New Testament were related to apostolic leaders. Paul told Titus to appoint elders in every city (see Titus 1:5). Titus gave the house-church elders apostolic oversight and served on Paul's leadership team.

Timing is paramount when it comes to finding an apostolic leader who can provide oversight to a new house-church network. I (Larry) have friends who lived on the South Island of New Zealand and who experienced faulty apostolic leadership because they did not wait on God's timing. In my friends' house church, there was a move of God that was so powerful that dozens of people came to faith in Christ and became a part of their house church within just a few months. With the increase in attendance, the leaders of the house church saw the need for connection to others in the Body of Christ and for spiritual oversight.

Around that same time, my friends heard about a new "apostle" who was coming to town and they assumed they should join with him and the house churches to which he was giving oversight. It did not take long, however, for them to discover that this "apostle" was a wolf in sheep's clothing—and because he was not under anyone's authority, they had no one to turn to. Within months, God's precious work in my friends' house church was in shambles because of the abusive "apostle." Paul warns us in 2 Corinthians 11:13 against false apostles who are not fathers but have a personal agenda. As my friends' example makes clear, house churches must take time to pray and discern as they seek God's direction for spiritual oversight.

In situations that require waiting on God's timing for apostolic oversight, leadership may come from the spiritual leader of a community church or mega-church in the area. We know of several instances in America where partnerships between house churches and community or mega-churches have worked well.

The Role of the Five Equipping Gifts

Paul describes five spiritual gifts that have been given to people to equip the Church for ministry:

> It was he who gave some to be apostles, some to be prophets, some to be evangelists, and some to be pas-

tors and teachers, to prepare God's people for works of service, so that the body of Christ may be built up (Eph. 4:11-12).

We especially like the way the *New Living Translation* translates verse 12: "Their responsibility is to equip God's people to do his work and build up the church, the body of Christ."

People with these spiritual gifts are placed in the Church to serve as spiritual fathers and mothers, called to equip and strengthen other followers of Jesus to do the work God has given them. The Greek word translated "train" or "prepare" is a medical term used to describe what happens when a doctor mends a broken leg, making it possible for a person to walk normally again. It's also the word used to describe the repair of a broken mast on a sailing vessel—when the two broken parts of the mast are joined and bound together, the mended mast is actually stronger than it was before. Similarly, God has placed teachers, pastors, apostles, prophets and evangelists in the Church to mend broken people so that they can walk and journey for the Lord. He gives these people so that we are encouraged and empowered to be all God wants us to be.

Men and women who exercise spiritual gifts speak with the Lord's authority—they represent different aspects of the ministry of the Lord Jesus when He was on the earth. Like the rest of us, they must earn the influence they have in people's lives through godly character, wisdom and living a life of spiritual devotion and discipline. The Lord validates them by the evidence of spiritual fruit, changed lives and the way He works supernaturally through them. They are recognized by local church leadership and released into ministry. But how does it happen? How do these spiritually gifted leaders grow in the first place?

An individual's gifts and abilities first become apparent when that person serves others, allows God to shape his or her character, and lives as a committed, accountable member of a community of people who love and obey Jesus. Once these people are recognized, they are given greater responsibility. Ideally, those who are older and more mature mentor those who are younger, and those who are gifted in a particular area mentor those with the same gifts. Through these practices, a multiplication of gifts and ministries takes place in the Church.

Of the many who are gifted as evangelists, apostles and so forth, our understanding is that most are not intended by God to be used solely in one house church or congregation (see Acts 15:22,30-32,35). Hopefully, those people with spiritual abilities will be recognized and encouraged to have a wide sphere of influence in the Church.[8] A powerful example of this principle are the circuit riders of John Wesley's Methodist house churches. These circuit riding preachers were the spiritual specialists who traveled from small church to small church in England and in America, keeping the Methodist movement connected and growing.

Apostles, Prophets, Evangelists, Pastors and Teachers Help the Church Mature

Apostles are given to the Church as bearers of a vision from the Lord that helps us to reach the whole world. Prophets are given to train us to listen to the voice of God. Evangelists are called to stir and train us to reach those who don't know Jesus. Pastors are commissioned to encourage and show us how to make disciples and care for people. Teachers have a divinely given ability to help us love, study and obey the Word of God. The church that has a balanced input from people with each of these gifts is the church that wants to grow.

House churches, because they are small, need to work extra hard to make sure they have a balanced diet of people with all five of these spiritual gifts. Take the gift of evangelism, for example. If your house church is lacking in a zeal for evangelism, ask an evangelist to come and minister to you for a few weeks. Ask him or her to not only teach about evangelism but also to take people out on the streets to share their faith. You will be amazed at the results! Consider blessing these ministry specialists with monetary gifts and love offerings to support their ongoing ministries.

Many pastors of community churches or mega-churches prefer to do the preaching and teaching themselves each Sunday, but house-church leaders must think differently. They must look for specialists in the Body of Christ who can add into the house church any spiritual gifts that the group is missing so that members will grow strong and mature in the faith.

Notes
1. A. M. Stibbs and A. F. Walls, *First Peter, Tyndale New Testament Commentaries* (Leicester, England: InterVarsity Press, 1983), p. 109.
2. See also 1 Timothy 3:1-7.
3. For more on this vital subject, see Larry Kreider, Ron Myer, Steve Prokopchak and Brian Sauder, *The Biblical Role of Elders for Today's Church* (Lititz, PA: House to House Publications, 2004).
4. Peter Bunton, *Cell Groups and House Churches: What History Teaches Us* (Lititz, PA: House to House Publications, 2001).
5. Larry Kreider, *House to House* (Lititz, PA: House to House Publications, 1995).
6. Peter Bunton, *Cell Groups and House Churches: What History Teaches Us* (Lititz, PA: House to House Publications, 2001).
7. Floyd McClung, *The Father Heart of God* (Eugene, OR: Harvest House Publishers, 1985), pp. 129-131.
8. For a more comprehensive biblical understanding of how the fivefold ministries effectively serve house churches and conventional churches, we encourage you to read *Fivefold Ministry Made Practical* by Ron Myer (Lititz, PA: House to House Publications, 2005).

CHAPTER 14

PITFALLS TO AVOID

By now you should realize that we are advocates of house church! We are completely convinced that God will lead thousands of people to start new house churches within the next few years.

That could be good or it could be a disaster. House church is not a panacea for all that ails the institutional Church, nor should it be an end in itself. Like any church, house churches can get off track—every church is made up of fallen people who hurt and disappoint each other. We make mistakes. We sin. The closer we get to each other, the more we see each other's faults and the more we can hurt each other. Relational Christianity in house churches can be messy. Here are some common pitfalls and how to overcome them.

The Pitfall of Consumer Christianity

House church should be about something far more radical than trying to be a smaller version of big churches. If we simply replicate the bigger churches we know well (on a smaller scale), we end up multiplying problems, not offering solutions. Our culture needs a new expression of church, not a dumbed-down mini-version of what already exists. If people want a church that is radically committed to the mission of God, sooner or later they will have to contend with the values— the DNA, if you will—that have been instilled in them for years in traditional churches.

Many Americans and Europeans have a consumer approach to church, and when they become part of a house church, they default to focusing on their own needs and the needs of their children and teenagers, rather than seeing themselves as the servants of the Kingdom. There is an inability on the part of most Christians in America and Europe to define church in truly Biblical terms. It is vital for them to be able to define what church is and is not—to define the difference between the biblical essence of church and the cultural forms in which it comes packaged.

DNA is an apt analogy for the persistence of values imported into house churches from traditional churches. The problem we face is almost cellular! Apple trees produce apples and orange trees produce oranges, and if a person's experience has been a social, cultural and economic system that produces churches shaped by our Western culture, we should not expect that person to produce anything different without deep spiritual—*cellular*—change.

Leaders of all church sizes know what it's like for people to leave over a slight disagreement about the style of worship or for a different variety of programs offered at another church. Many Americans and Europeans choose their church like they pick toothpaste—by shopping! If they don't like the product at one church, they'll check out another product the next week. House churches run counter to this consumer mentality. They flat-out don't work unless people are committed.

The Pitfall of Inauthentic Community

If we seek community with other followers of Jesus without an orientation to a new definition of church—a definition that is about genuine community and radical commission—people will revert to expectations based on older models. We must orient people to a community based on genuine relationships that require honesty, forgiveness and mercy. If we do not, churches will experience conflict and division among people, and conflicting expectations within people.

House church must be about authentic community in order to be relevant to our culture. Biblical house church is about family—something we all desperately want but aren't generally good at doing. Unless we address this issue up front with answers from the Bible, many house churches will struggle with problems of disunity and unfulfilled expectations.

In order to experience genuine community in a house church, we have to trust other people . . . but there is this little problem called sin! We don't, however, believe that sin is the greatest barrier to community, but lack of forgiveness. People in our nation are broken, and trust doesn't come easy these days. When people consider whether or not to trust, many seem to think that the *other* person's sinfulness is the problem. They are idealistic about their own lack of sin. Idealists don't do well in community—not because they are imperfect, but because they don't acknowledge their imperfections and received the forgiveness of God. If idealists have not received forgiveness, they will struggle with giving it to others.

It's important to get this right. If you are part of a small community, sooner or later someone will do something to hurt or disappoint you, and you may once again have good reason to avoid "the Church." But Dietrich Bonhoeffer points out in his book *Life Together* that the Church is not a place for idealists and humanists. Rather, Church is a community of forgiven sinners, a family of people who need mercy from those who have learned to forgive like Jesus.

The Pitfall of Pride

A common pitfall in any new, radical effort to do church differently is pride. Pioneers of new church communities may tend to view their way of doing church as the one and only solution for

today's ailing Christian culture. If we are doing church differently because it is novel, because it is trendy or because it meets
some personal need or preference, we are doing it for the wrong
reasons. Simple church communities are only one of many
ways the Lord is calling the Church to rise up and be unleashed
in the world today. One model does not fit all.

As soon as we think our group is the only "right" group
around town, we're in trouble. Pride always comes before a
fall. We must learn to follow the path the Lord has laid out for
us with great conviction and, at the same time, honor what
He is doing through others walking a path that looks different from our own.

If you have been turned off by those involved in house
churches because of their bad attitudes or unwelcoming spirits,
please don't throw the baby out with the bathwater. House-
church groups should be forewarned that when they take on
the mentality that their group is the best ("Us four, no more!"),
they are on dangerous ground. We must guard against a "house
church vs. organized church" mentality in which we view traditional church structures as inferior.

If any kind of church (community, mega- or house)
becomes exclusive in its thinking, it has derailed. We are all
a part of the worldwide Body of Christ. There is only one
Church, and we must make every effort to walk in unity. God
has placed us in a particular church so that we may grow deep
in a given place with a community of people. The issue is not
which church is best—every church family has strengths and
weaknesses. The issue is this: Where has God placed you?
Which group of believers has the Lord called you to work with
during this season of your life? Find that church, and plant
yourself there. Put down roots. Grow with others in the same
community. Don't run from problems and don't avoid problem people.

The Pitfall of Fear

Another trap to avoid is fear, particularly fear of what people think. House churches are largely unproven entities in today's church world. They are new to many people and depend upon sometimes-inexperienced people to provide leadership. Despite these challenges, house-church leaders must act in faith, not in fear. They must build what God has called them to build and gain the courage to press on even when they encounter people who question their nontraditional approach to church. Even though house churches may lack credibility, what they lack in status can be made up for by courage and vision.

Fear of our own mistakes is another thing that can hinder us. Bible teacher Bob Mumford once said, "I do not trust anyone unless he walks with a limp." He was referring to Genesis 32, when Jacob, after wrestling with the Lord and demanding His blessing, was touched in his thigh and from that day forward, walked with a limp. When God lovingly deals with us through difficult times, we walk with a spiritual limp the rest of our lives. This is the stuff of which true spiritual fathers and mothers are made.

Peter, the disciple who became an apostle of the New Testament church is another example of a spiritual father with a spiritual limp. After denying Jesus and then experiencing His complete acceptance and forgiveness, Peter lost his abrasiveness and became a true father in the faith. From that time on he "walked with a limp."

Both Jacob's and Peter's examples testify to the fact that we all make mistakes. They also teach us that we must not give up. We may be doing all the right things, but problems will still arise. Or we may be tempted to go back to something easier than dealing with the shortcomings of humanity. Being a spiritual parent to believers in a house church is not easy. But it *is* rewarding.

The Bible says that all things are possible, not that all things are easy! Even Jesus dealt with problems while investing His life in the 12 disciples. They all left Him in the Garden of Gethsemane. He felt alone and forsaken. But He knew that the last chapter was not yet written! Fifty days later, Peter stood with the 11 and preached at Pentecost, where 3,000 people came to faith in Christ. No doubt, Jesus was just as proud of fearful Peter preaching to a multitude as He was to see thousands believe in Him.

The Pitfall of an Independent Spirit

Still another hidden danger is developing an independent and isolationist spirit. Sometimes those who do not want to be under any type of spiritual authority gravitate toward house churches because they believe they can do their own thing without having to answer to anyone. There are also house-church groups that are reactionary against the institutional Church, often indicative that people have been hurt or abused in traditional churches by controlling leaders.

Through this kind of disillusionment and disappointment, believers may totally isolate themselves from the greater Church. This kind of independent spirit is a form of pride, and it is very unhealthy. In contrast, the Lord's plan is to use the local church to protect us, help us grow and equip us to be all that we can be in Jesus Christ.

Another example of an independent-spirited house church is one we've all heard of: the group of people who have been together for years and haven't grown at all. This kind of ingrown Christianity has forgotten about people who don't know Christ!

We must never lose sight of the truth that we are all part of the same Body and we exist to bring others into the Kingdom. We must never cut ourselves off from other believers or the people around us who desperately need the love of Jesus.

The Pitfall of Heresy

House churches may fall into the trap of heresy if they are exclusive and unwilling to work with others. This can be avoided if we are accountable to other leaders in a house-church network and in the Body of Christ at large. We need accountability to keep us from false teaching.

New expressions of the Church are sometimes unnecessarily persecuted as heretical simply because they have a new way of looking at things and are structured differently. Early Reformer Martin Luther persecuted the Anabaptists and had them put in prison because they practiced adult believer's baptism. The Reformers were guilty of persecuting the Baptists, who in turn persecuted the Pentecostals. Some of our Assembly of God pastor friends lament their persecution of the Charismatic movement of the 1960s and 1970s because of their break with traditional Pentecostalism. Needless to say, all church traditions are guilty of reacting negatively to the "new kid on the block."

The best solution to heresy in the Church is *not* to have better-trained leaders in the pulpits, but to have better-trained people in the pews. An institutionalized church does not keep us from error. The size and structure of the church does not keep us from heresy. We can only find freedom from error by testing everything by the Word of God, in relationship with godly believers outside our circle and accountable to others in the wider Body of Christ.

Matt Green, editor of *Ministry Today*, says that we cannot worry about "the theological pitfalls faced by devout believers exploring the scriptures and worshipping in the privacy of their own home . . . house churches are the least likely seedbeds of heresy . . . they are the natural offspring of the Reformation's cry: *Ecclesia reformata, semper reformanda* ('The church reformed and always to be reformed')."[1]

An ecclesiastical elite should not preserve doctrine. Doctrine must be articulated, taught, transmitted and understood by ordinary, everyday believers. In house churches, each believer is encouraged to understand the basic tenets of sound Christian doctrine as taught in the Scriptures and to assume responsibility for the spiritual health of themselves and the other members.

Neil Cole of Church Multiplication Associates, a family of simple church networks, explains how they handle the threat of heresy in simple church:

> Do I teach Scriptural interpretive skills in our movement? Yes, I do, but it is not the first thing I do. First I set the saints to reading the Scripture without any middleman. Once the sheep hear the Good Shepherd's voice they will follow Him for life. There is a significant "imprinting" that needs to take place from the very beginning of a new life. Like the baby ducks that will follow their mother, new disciples must connect with God's voice early on.
>
> People will ask me, "Then aren't the disciples going to misunderstand Scripture?" Yes, of course they are. And so did I when I was a young disciple. Perhaps we should allow people the freedom to make a few mistakes, leave with a few questions, and learn as they grow. I remember my first Bible study that I ever taught—it was heresy! And I managed to utter a four-letter word in it as well. I am glad someone gave me a chance to do better the next time.
>
> I do teach basic Bible interpretation skills, but I wait until the disciples emerge as leaders and are preparing to teach others. When they are responsible for others' learning, then I teach them basic interpretive skills. But here is the amazing thing: when I teach interpretive skills for the first time to a new leader it is usually a

refresher course for them. Because they have been reading an abundance of Scripture from the beginning, and
reading entire books of the Bible repetitively and as a
whole, they have already picked up much of the rules of
interpretation intuitively. I have found that the Holy
Spirit is an outstanding teacher and that the best inter-
pretive rules are really common sense. By the time I am
showing these rules to emerging leaders they have already
figured out much of it on their own.[2]

The Pitfall of Forgetting the Great Commission

Jesus tells us in Matthew 28:19-20:

> Therefore go and make disciples of all nations, baptizing
> them in the name of the Father and of the Son and of the
> Holy Spirit, and teaching them to obey everything I have
> commanded you. And surely I am with you always, to the
> very end of the age.

This is not only the main purpose of house-church ministry
but also the calling of the whole Church. We are all called to
obey and fulfill the Great Commission.

It is so easy to forget the primary purpose for the Church, and
even when we do remember, we easily lose sight of the chief objec-
tive for the Great Commission: for Jesus to receive more glory, *not*
for more people to get saved. The ultimate goal of all creation is
to glorify God and enjoy Him forever by loving and obeying Him.

The Pitfall of Discouragement

Getting involved in a house church can be discouraging. Why?
Because it's not like going to a mega-church where everything

is done for you. You are not a spectator, but an active participant. It is a community to belong to, not a set of doctrines to believe about Church. In the early stages, it is new and fun. Then comes a stage of involvement, which is about going deeper in relationships, working through personality differences and learning to open up your life honestly in ways that may be difficult for you, even threatening.

Then comes the stage that is the biggest challenge: realizing that you are responsible. Everyone has to accept responsibility for what happens—otherwise, things don't happen. Things won't get fixed unless everyone shoulders the load.

At this stage, many battle the temptation to quit. The enemy may try to use discouragement to take you out of the game. In a sense, you are a pioneer, and pioneers pay a price while others receive the benefits. Someone built the highway in your city, but now you drive down it without even thinking about the massive sacrifice someone made to build it.

One thing that may add to the battle of wanting to quit is being—at least initially—misunderstood. When we (Larry and LaVerne) started small groups in our new church plant in 1980, many Christians in our community thought we were crazy. (As it turned out, it was not easy.) During the spring of 1992, I was ready to quit. I felt misunderstood, and I wasn't sure if it was worth all the hassle. I told LaVerne one day, "If I get kicked in the head one more time, figuratively speaking, I don't know if I can get up again."

As the senior leader of our church, I was frustrated, exhausted and overworked. God had given me a vision to build the underground church, but over the course of a few years we had strayed from that original vision. My immaturity as a leader, lack of training and my own inability to communicate clearly the things God was showing me led to my frustration. In a misguided attempt to please everyone, I listened to dozens of voices, each of which seemed to give conflicting advice and direction. I felt unable to get back on track.

Finally, I was encouraged to take a sabbatical. During the last few weeks of that needed break, I spent some extended time at a cabin in the mountains. One morning I went out for a jog, and in a totally unexpected way, I had an encounter with the living God. The following is an excerpt of what I recorded in my journal:

I had an amazing spiritual experience this morning. I went out for a jog and took an unfamiliar road. I came upon a creek that crossed the road, and my jogging came to a screeching halt. I was ready to turn around and go back when I heard a still, small voice within me saying, "Take your shoes off and cross over the creek barefooted."

I sensed that the Lord was asking me to take a step of obedience and faith and cross over the creek. This was not only a natural creek; it also had deep spiritual significance for my life and for DOVE Christian Fellowship. The Lord was asking me to cross the creek in faith and in humility and allow the water to wash away all of the hurts, expectations, fears, insecurities and ways of doing things from the past so that the Lord could teach me fresh and anew for the future.

As I took this step of obedience, I sensed that others who are called to serve with me in leadership will need to do the same thing spiritually—walk in humility and allow the Holy Spirit to wash them clean of many of the hurts, mind-sets and expectations of the past. The Lord has called us from the wilderness to the promised land of Canaan. We must forget what is behind and press on to what the Lord has for us in the future.

The Lord's desire, as I understand it, is for us to move on from a Moses mentality to a Joshua mentality. Moses and the people of God walked "in a circle" for 40 years. Joshua had a clear mandate from the Lord to go into the Promised Land and take it back from the enemy. Moses majored on maintenance while Joshua led an army! Each member of the army had clear areas to champion and to conquer, but they were all committed to walk together to fulfill the purposes of the Lord.

* * *

As I continued on, I walked past a home where two dogs barked at me, one on either side of the road. One was quite a ferocious looking beast. I just spoke gently and walked on by, and it hit me that there was certainly nothing to fear. Both of these dogs were chained and could bark and make all of the noise that they wanted, but they could not touch me or harm me in any way.

As we take steps of faith, there will be some "dogs barking" (words spoken—harshly, perhaps—against us), but they don't matter because the enemy cannot touch us. God knows our hearts and He will vindicate.

As I continued to walk, it was as if a whole new world were opening up before me. The fields were beautiful and it was sheer delight to walk along these country roads. I had a clear sense that I was walking in the right direction, but in reality, it was a real step of faith—the road was entirely unfamiliar to me. I believe that this is symbolic of the future. We walk in the direction that we believe the Lord wants us to walk, and have to totally trust the precious Holy Spirit for direction—and as we trust, there is a tremendous sense of peace.

* * *

The next thing that happened, I see as extremely significant. I passed an old church building. A new building was being built on the backside of the property. People were hustling and bustling around, working together on this project. What was so amazing to me was that the workers were women, teens and men, all joyfully working together to fulfill a common purpose—to build the new church building. I felt the excitement and the joy and the expectancy within the people as I walked by.

Just as these people were working together to build a physical building, the Lord is calling together a company of His people to work together to build His spiritual building. In the same way that these workers were inexperienced in the eyes of the world, the Lord will use those who may appear to be inexperienced in the eyes of the Church to build His spiritual house. These workers were using new lumber to build this building, and the Lord is going to require us to use new lumber (new Christians) in the building of this spiritual house.

I believe that the Lord has wonderful plans for those who are willing to forget the past and press on to what the Lord has in the future. Sure enough, the road that I traveled by faith brought me back to the cabin. I now had renewed faith and vitality to press forward in the calling God had given to me years ago—to be involved in building the underground church. I had crossed the river.

If you believe that the Lord may be calling you to labor with Him to build His Church according to the principles that are outlined in this book, you will probably have to cross your own river. After you cross, there is no turning back. But then, who wants to go back to the wilderness? Let's march like Joshua, through the river, with a confidence that the Lord is saving the best wine for last. He is waiting for you and me to prepare the wineskins so that He can pour out His Spirit, from house to house, city to city and nation to nation.

Notes
1. Matt Green, "Heretics @ Home? Are House Churches Really More Vulnerable to False Doctrine?" *Ministries Today,* June 7, 2006.
2. Neil Cole, "The Threat of Heresy in the Organic Church Movement," DAWN Ministries archives, www.dawnministries.org.

CHAPTER 15

HOUSE, COMMUNITY AND MEGA-CHURCHES WORKING TOGETHER

Some time back, I (Floyd) was alone in a guest room at a Bible school. I had some free time between lectures and I decided to read through the book of Ephesians for a devotional. As I read, I reflected on the great apostle's words in Ephesians 3:10, when he wrote, "The manifold wisdom of God might be made known by the church." I tried to understand what the words meant. I looked up the meaning of the word *manifold*: "varied, many different kinds, having many parts." The question that followed for me was, How could a perfect God make known the many and varied aspects of His greatness through imperfect people?

As I struggled with what Paul was describing to the Ephesians, I had a distinct impression of God speaking to my mind, like one of those silent conversations we have with ourselves. I know this sounds far-fetched, but I sensed God speaking these words to me: "This is My greatness, to make Myself known through the people who are My Church." It didn't make sense to me, but I knew that what I was hearing was one of the greatest things I would ever learn about God. I reflected on the implications of what He was speaking to my heart and then He spoke to me again: "That I reveal myself through broken, fallen people is a revelation of the God I am."

Slowly, the revelation grew in my mind. I had seen plenty of the Church's problems, but God seemed to be saying to me that it is actually part of His plan to make Himself known through broken, weak people. I began to understand for the very first time that God invites us to partner with Him in revealing His love to others. That He chooses to partner with us—even though we are sinful—is a sign of His greatness. I am still stunned by God's humility and kindness. That He invites me to be a coworker in sharing His love with others never ceases to amaze me.

Obviously, this throws new light on the nature of the Church and what it is about. We are a community of forgiven sinners, and the Church will sometimes disappoint because it is made up of people. But it is also a community of forgiven people—people who acknowledge their imperfections and receive forgiveness and grace. Churches in general, and house churches in particular, may be a little messy around the edges, but they are movements that are infiltrating society, alive with the love of Jesus, sent by God Himself.

The Church of today is a diverse one, and diversity is healthy. God is working through program-designed churches, cell-based churches, community churches, mega-churches and house-church networks. Working together keeps us accountable to each other. Although we work differently, those who love Jesus and who are passionate about His glory filling the earth are allies in the same cause.

Working Together as the "Big C" Church

We have described three types of churches: one like a local grocery store, one like a Wal-Mart superstore, and one like the stores in a mall. There is the small, simple church, the medium-sized community church, and the huge mega-church. All three kinds of churches can work together to impact their city for God. We are not thinking in terms of forming a super-church, with one name and governed by one set of leaders. Rather, we are thinking of the churches in a city or region from God's per-spective—as the "Big C" Church. He sees all the believers as His children, His spiritual family.

The heart of the Scriptures teaches us that it is the Lord's desire for us to experience the building and expansion of His kingdom in our particular region of the world (see Matt. 6:33). We envision the Body of Christ working together in organized yet informal ways across a city or region. In some instances, community churches and mega-churches may commission some of their leaders to start house churches and give them the oversight needed to help them grow. We believe commu-nity churches and mega-churches will increasingly "adopt" house churches into their communities and help them net-work together. Other community churches will commission future house-church leaders to join with networks in their region. I (Floyd) am close to Harvest Church in Port Elizabeth, South Africa. This is a mega-church that is following the Lord's challenge to their leaders to "give the church back to the people." In an orderly yet uncontrolling way, the leaders of Harvest Church are encouraging the planting of both commu-nity and house churches. Mega-churches in other locations can learn much from the example of Harvest Church and it's commitment to advance God's kingdom by giving the church back to the people.

Even though most house churches will continue to birth new house churches, some of these small, simple churches may actually become community churches—and some of these com-munity churches could become mega-churches! It's all up to the commander-in-chief of the Church, the Lord Jesus Christ. There is tremendous freedom in the kingdom of God!

It is also possible that some people may be in a house-church network for a season and then be called by God to become involved in a community church or a mega-church.

We must remember that it is the entire Church in each of our regions that matters. We believe in the kind of freedom that encourages God's people to serve wherever God has called them. What is most important is that people are planted and put their roots down deep in the church God calls them to be part of.

Humility and Unity

During the industrial age, adults usually kept the same job their entire lives. In today's information age, however, studies show that the average person will make at least five career changes during the course of a lifetime. Today's society is a mobile one, which forces us to be flexible. This same principle applies in church life.

Each kind of church has its strengths and weaknesses as it endeavors to empower people for ministry. Some new believers may be initially discipled in house churches but may eventually become involved in a community church or a mega-church—or vice-versa. Therefore, we believe it is important to keep open and friendly relationships with others in church structures that are different from ours. Respect, born out of humility, is the key for building God's kingdom.

We believe that the Lord is doing an awesome thing in our day. He is restoring the unity He prayed for in John 17:21: "That all of them may be one, Father, just as you are in me and I am in you. May they also be in us so that the world may believe that you have sent me." Walls that have divided denominations and churches for centuries are coming down throughout the world at an increasing rate. Pastors in the same town who never knew one another are now finding each other, praying together regularly and supporting each other. This kind of Church unity is exciting!

The Church in Your Region

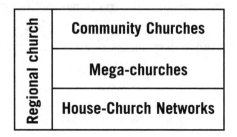

Six years ago, the senior pastor and elder team of our (Larry and LaVerne's) community church, DOVE Westgate, gave their blessing to our involvement in coaching a new micro-church network in our area. The LMCN agreed to be our overseer. We opened our home for a micro-church on Wednesday evenings and when I am not traveling on the weekends, I worship at DOVE Westgate on Sunday mornings with LaVerne.

Duane Britton, the senior pastor of DOVE Westgate, and Mike Stoltzfus, who heads up the LMCN, are friends. They are both secure leaders. Only secure leaders can handle this type of flexibility.

Some of the new believers in our house church have joined us some Sunday mornings in our community church. They appreciate the worship experience and the Bible teaching. There have been other house-church members who felt led by the Lord to leave our house church and join a local community church. Even others joined a mega-church. We want to bless those who are led to move on to other churches and we want to stay in good relationship with them. Remember, all three types of churches are being used by the Lord to serve His people.

Church unity among community churches, mega-churches and house-church networks makes room for the Church in your region to emerge. What does this Church look like? We believe it will be comprised of all types of churches—community churches, mega-churches, house churches, Baptists, Methodists and Charismatics—all working together in a particular geographical area. These churches, of many different types and denominations, represent the Church (the Body of Christ) as they honor one another, pray for each other and speak well of each other in a city or region.

In the New Testament, each church was identified by its geographical location—there were no denominations back then! The Body of Christ met in house churches within a city, and they were unified by their specific city boundaries: the church of Antioch, the church of Corinth, the church of Jerusalem, the church of Smyrna. Today, however, the Church has been divided into many different denominations within one geographical area. Many times, such things as doctrinal interpretations and worship styles are the cause of these divisions in the Body of Christ.

Our desire for churches to come together in unity in our regions is not an attempt to do away with denominations and get back to distinguishing believers on the sole basis of geography. On the contrary, we believe that we have to work with what we have. This means that the local churches within a collective regional church will probably maintain their denominational flavors while working in a unified manner to more effectively share Christ in their area. In short, we believe that when unbelievers see the unity of churches in their communities, they will be more attracted to following Christ.

Our Father has called us to become one as He and His Son are one. This type of unity is costly in terms of time, relationship building and resource sharing, and it must come from the heart. When it happens, it is a powerful force for attracting people to Jesus.

Spiritual Parents Working Together Regionally

Our prayer and hope is that men and women who are spiritual fathers and mothers will work together to serve the Church. I (Floyd) have seen this happen on several occasions. Baptist pastor Bob Spradley leads the citywide prayer movement in Kansas City, and he is the kind of man that any leader with an ounce of humility can follow. He leads weekly, monthly and annual prayer events that have had a huge impact on the city. Bob's example of wisdom, passion for Jesus and love for those who don't know Jesus has been inspirational to many pastors in Kansas City.

We believe it is on God's heart for this type of unity to happen in every city and region of our nation. We would go so far as to say that we believe there will be an emergence of spiritual leaders from various backgrounds and denominations who will form teams of spiritual leadership to promote and serve the Church in various towns, cities and rural areas of our country. They will not think only in terms of pastoring a church or churches, but will work and pray with fellow servant-leaders in the Body of Christ to pastor their region.

These initiatives will not be contrary to a person's denominational distinctiveness, but will bring blessing to the Church in a given region. What we are describing is already happening on a national scale through networks of churches led by Bill Hybels and the Willow Creek Associa-tion, Rick Warren and the PEACE initiative and the Acts 29 network out of Mars Hill Church in Seattle. Men and women of different denominations are networking together in ways we would not have thought possible in the past to provide resources for one another and help each other plant more churches.

Although these movements are concerned with unity, unity is not their primary focus. Their main focus is on the mandate that the Church has already received: to reach those who do not know Jesus and to impact our culture in relevant ways by bringing God's message to the world. What we have yet to see are networks formed on citywide and regional levels. When this happens, we will see churches empowering one another to engage our culture with the good news of Jesus.

An Example of Regional Church Unity

This kind of unity is beginning among the churches in our (Larry and LaVerne's) region of Lancaster County, Pennsylvania. During the past few years, a local regional Christian leadership group has emerged and is in place to empower the Church in its many expressions (www.theregionalchurch.com). This group has a vision to "see the church maturing in Christ, strategically serving together to revitalize the Church, give a Christ-centered witness to each resident, and bring transformation to the way of life in this region.[3] Hundreds of leaders in our county are committed to working together as a leadership community, regardless of their affiliation. They represent church leadership, ministry leadership and Christians in leadership in the marketplace—pastors, teachers, doctors, legislators, psychiatrists, counselors, ministry leaders, artists, authors, corporate CEOs and business professionals. This regional group is not an organization to join, but an organized network of leaders devoted to relationships.

Through prayer and fasting, they have appointed 20 leaders to work together on a council to serve the Christian leadership community. Council members include key ministry leaders and Christian leaders from many types of churches. Some are members of community churches, others are members of mega-churches, while others are members of new house-church networks. All are members of the Body of Christ in our region.

This regional team is committed to cooperatively establishing the kingdom of God in the home, neighborhood, community and marketplace. When the Body of Christ joins in unity like this, we believe we are bound to see results! One regional member astutely remarked:

> The Regional Church of Lancaster County represents a very special time in the history of Lancaster County. Churches and ministries from a variety of persuasions are coming together, not as an ecumenical movement but as a God-led movement, to see our county impacted by Jesus Christ Himself.

This effort is an attempt to help coordinate and serve, rather than control, the work of God in our region. Cooperative efforts must always take on this perspective. We are certainly not yet in revival, but the Lord has brought down walls that for generations had been erected between churches and denominations.

We believe God calls Christians from community churches, mega-churches and house-church networks to serve together as the Church in every region of every city, in every nation. Together, we can reach the world.

Downsizing in Order to Grow

"Downsizing" is a familiar term to corporations that face increasingly stiff competition in the global economy. Corporations that downsize are trying to rid themselves of unessential costs and liabilities. They may, for example, downsize their work force or inventory in order to cut unnecessary costs. Downsizing is one way that corporations can continue to exist and expect to be profitable.

Similarly, community churches, mega-churches and house churches in a region would do well to work together to use all their resources more fully. Why not "downsize" by sharing resources? We believe that churches of all sizes, like corporations, will discover myriads of ways that they can rid themselves of unessential costs and liabilities.

For example, we look forward to the day when we can be so flexible that we will allow church buildings in our communities to be used every day of the week. Many community churches and mega-churches currently use their buildings for a few chosen meetings (Sunday morning worship service, midweek prayer meeting, etc.), and the church facility remains unused the rest of the week. If our paradigm changed and churches banded together to build community centers that served members of the community and not just the church attendees, the Church would be viewed differently.

Or how about this scenario: A community church or mega-church offers or rents its facility to several different house-church networks that want to meet in a larger setting each month. The various congregations sharing the facility could have their weekly or monthly celebrations at different times during the week. The leaders of the traditional church could partner with the leaders of the house-church network to form a joint outreach team that would brainstorm how to turn the facility into a center for community-based sports programs, Boy and Girl Scout troops, adult education, family enrichment, 12-step programs and so on—and the Church would once again be the center of activity in the community! DOVE Christian Fellowship in Pennsylvania is about to launch some new house churches that will come together monthly in the building of a local church that is not part of the DOVE family, so we know this model of facility sharing can work. When churches share buildings, the money that is saved on constructing new buildings and maintaining old buildings can be given to missions, to the poor and to serve the community at large.

LaVerne and I (Larry) are a part of an awesome house church that meets every week in a home in Lancaster County. We have a blast each week eating, praying, and reaching out to pre-Christians together, and serving one another in practical ways. We also try to find ways to serve the more traditional churches in our community. When a group of churches in our region were unable to raise all the money needed to give to a group of missionaries and international church leaders, our house church made the decision to give a few thousand dollars to help them.

Is it asking too much for churches in a given area to work together to serve their city or community like this? Perhaps we have taken the simple gospel and the simple ways of doing church and complicated them. We are calling the Church to get back to its calling, to serve the community and to share earthly goods as well as the good news with others.

Churches That Honor Each Other

When LaVerne and I (Larry) were married in 1971, we found that we had two sets of relationships to pursue and maintain: those on her side of the family and those on mine. Both were important.

In the same way, every church leader needs to maintain healthy relationships with the fathers of their church movement *and* with the spiritual fathers in their town, city or region. When the Ford Corporation runs a car through the assembly line in Detroit, the parts have been gathered from companies all over the world. Similarly, God has brought the Church in the U.S. together from around the world. He has taken the unique mix of people, culture, denominations and church families and has assembled them in your city.

As we cultivate an attitude of love and respect for the different "parts" in our region, the Lord will bless us. Psalm 133 says that God "has pronounced his blessing, even life forevermore" on those who live together in harmony (*NLT*). If you study revivals in Church history, you will find that one of the most important prerequisites to experiencing God's blessing is unity among pastors and church leaders.

A New Model for a New Time

Second Kings 4:1-7 tells the story of Elisha and how he miraculously multiplied the oil of a poor widow. As long as the widow had vessels to pour the oil into, the flow of oil continued. When she ran out of vessels, the supply of new oil was halted. In many ways, this story is a picture of the Church. God has promised to pour out His Holy Spirit, but His pouring necessitates flexible containers to hold the great harvest that is on the horizon. Is it possible that the Lord is waiting for His Church to prepare the proper containers so that He can fully pour out His Spirit?

The effective networking of new house churches in our communities will give the opportunity for thousands of new churches to be rapidly planted across our nation and in the nations of the world. Many more new churches are needed to care for the harvest of people coming into God's kingdom. We do not need fewer churches in our communities—we need more! Remember, only 17 percent of Americans regularly attend church in our nation. At the present rate of decline in church attendance, in a few years' time that number will be closer to 10 percent.

We believe that there are thousands of former pastors and Christian leaders who are no longer involved in church leadership because they have retired or are now working in the marketplace, unaware that they could be starting something smaller and less demanding than a structured, large church— they could be starting a brand-new church in their home.

Many people in our communities will not enter a church building, but they will come into our homes. Spiritual families led by humble spiritual moms and dads are not only a wave of the future—they are the present need!

Rick Joyner, a man God has used to challenge many of our "sacred cows," wrote that he believes a major awakening will soon occur within the Church, and that discerning leaders will be ready for it:

> A revolution is coming to Christianity that will eclipse the Reformation in the sweeping changes that it brings to the church. When it comes, the present structure and organization of the church will cease to exist, and the way that the world defines Christianity will be radically changed.
>
> What is coming will not be a change of doctrine, but a change in basic church life. The changes that are coming will be so profound that it will be hard to relate the present form of church structure and government to what is coming. The new dynamic of church life will overshadow the Great Awakenings in their social impact, transforming cities and even whole nations. It will bring a sweeping sense of righteousness and justice to the whole earth.
>
> The future leaders of the church are now being given a vision of radical New Testament Christianity being restored to the earth. It is time to heed the call and allow the Lord to lead His people to the new wineskins that will be able to hold what is about to break out upon the earth. Whenever there is a choice to make between the new and the old, choose the new. To be a part of what is coming, we must have the faith of Abraham, who was willing to leave the security of the known to seek God in unknown places. The future leaders of the church will be willing to risk all to seek the city that God is building, not man.[1]

We, too, believe that we must be open to the direction the Lord is leading us—toward new wineskins to hold the new wine that is about to be released upon the earth. We have the same sense of expectancy about the new house-church networks. Many future church leaders are sitting on church pews today, finding no room for their gifts to be released in their present structures. We must allow a radical kind of Christianity to break out and motivate our future leaders to action. House-church networks enable the priesthood of all believers, and require no expensive church buildings. It is our hope that every believer will realize his or her part to play in discipling the nations, and that mission-minded house churches will meet in every city and town until they cover our world with the good news of Jesus' love.

Note
1. Rick Joyner, "Revolution," *The Morning Star Prophetic Bulletin*, May 2000.

ABOUT THE AUTHORS

Larry Kreider is the founder and International Director of DOVE Christian Fellowship International (DCFI), an international family of cell and house churches that has successfully used the New Testament strategy of building the Church with small groups for more than 25 years. DOVE, an acronym for "Declaring Our Victory Emmanuel," started as a youth ministry in the late 1970s that targeted unchurched youth in south-central Pennsylvania. DCFI grew out of the ensuing need for a flexible New Testament-style church (new wineskin) that could assist these new believers (new wine). Today, the DCFI family consists of cell-based congregations and house churches that network throughout the United States, Central and South America, the Caribbean, Canada, Europe, Africa and the South Pacific.

Larry Kreider, International Director
DOVE Christian Fellowship International
11 Toll Gate Road
Lititz, PA 17543
Tel: (717) 627-1996
Fax: (717) 627-4004
www.dcfi.org
www.startingahousechurch.com

Floyd and Sally McClung live in Cape Town, South Africa, where they lead an outreach and training community. Their mission is to make disciples, train leaders and plant churches in Africa, Asia and other parts of the world. To learn more about Floyd and Sally and All Nations, visit their website at www.floydandsally.org and www.all-nations.info. Or you can write to Floyd personally at floyd.mcclung@gmail.com.

RESOURCES FROM DCFI

(WWW.DCFI.ORG)

The Cry for Spiritual Fathers and Mothers
Larry Kreider, 186 pages, $11.95, ISBN 1-886973-42-3
We must return to the biblical truth of spiritual parenting so
that believers are not left fatherless and disconnected. This
book shares how loving, seasoned spiritual fathers and mothers help spiritual children reach their potential.

Hearing God 30 Different Ways
Larry Kreider, 224 pages, $14.99, ISBN 1-886973-62-8
The Lord speaks to us in ways we often miss, including
through the Bible, prayer, circumstances, spiritual gifts, con-
viction, His character, His peace, and even in times of silence.
Take 30 days and, as you develop a loving relationship with
Him, discover how God's voice can become familiar to you.

The Biblical Role of Elders for Today's Church
Larry Kreider, Ron Myer, Steve Prokopchak and Brian Sauder
274 pages, $12.99, ISBN 1-886973-62-8
This book offers Testament principles for equipping church
leadership teams: Why leadership is needed, what their quali-
fications and responsibilities are, how they should be chosen,
how elders function as spiritual fathers and mothers, how
they are to make decisions, resolve conflicts, and more.

Biblical Foundation Series
Larry Kreider, each 64 pages, $4.99 each or
12-book set for $39, ISBN 1-886973-18-0
This series by Larry Kreider covers basic Christian doctrine.
Practical illustrations accompany the easy-to-understand format.

Use for small-group teachings (48 in all), a mentoring relationship or daily devotional. Titles include:

Knowing Jesus Christ as Lord

The New Way of Living

New Testament Baptisms

Building for Eternity

Living in the Grace of God

Freedom from the Curse

Learning to Fellowship with God

What Is the Church?

Authority and Accountability

God's Perspective on Finances

Called to Minister

The Great Commission

House to House
Larry Kreider, 206 pages, $8.95, ISBN 1-880828-81-2
This book follows the story of how DOVE Christian
Fellowship International has grown from a small fellowship
into a family of cell-based churches and house churches net-
working throughout the world.

Helping You Build Cell Churches manual
Compiled by Brian Sauder and Larry Kreider
224 pages, $19.95, ISBN: 1-886973-38-5
A complete biblical blueprint for cells, this manual covers 51
topics! This manual offers training to build cell churches from
the ground up. It includes study and discussion questions. Use
the manual for training cell leaders or for personal study.